Date: 10/29/19

153.852 HAN
Hanson, Jason
Agent of influence : how to
use spy skills to persuade

AGENT OF INFLUENCE

AGENT OF INFLUENCE

HOW TO USE SPY SKILLS TO PERSUADE ANYONE, SELL ANYTHING, AND BUILD A SUCCESSFUL BUSINESS

JASON HANSON

 DEY ST.
An Imprint of WILLIAM MORROW

DEY ST.

HarperCollins books may be purchased for educational, business, or sales promotional use. For information, please email the Special Markets Department at SPsales@harpercollins.com.

FIRST EDITION

Designed by Suet Chong
Art by Gerald Bernard/shutterstock

Library of Congress Cataloging-in-Publication Data has been applied for.

ISBN 978-0-06-289274-4

19 20 21 22 23 LSC 10 9 8 7 6 5 4 3 2 1

To all entrepreneurs and salesmen. The unsung heroes who help make America the greatest country on earth. And, to the incredibly brave men and women of the CIA who are the best salespeople on earth.

Opportunities will present themselves. Recognize them, act on them.

—Robert Ludlum, *The Bourne Supremacy*

AUTHOR'S NOTE

I am always grateful to the men and women from the CIA who share their stories with me, and I assured everyone I would protect their privacy. As you might imagine, privacy is of the utmost importance to those working in the intelligence field. For this reason, all the names and identifying details have been changed, and the stories have been edited for clarity and to ensure they would be understandable to people who do not work in the intelligence field. In some instances, dates and/ or geographical regions have been changed. Again, this was critical to do to ensure the privacy of everyone who joined me in this book.

CONTENTS

AGENT OF INFLUENCE

SPY SKILLS ARE GREAT BUSINESS SKILLS

From the very first day an intelligence officer begins his training, he is primed on how to become the best salesperson in the world. Spies aren't selling an ordinary product, however. The product they're selling is treason. If an intelligence officer doesn't close a deal, he might end up getting killed or spending the rest of his life inside a foreign prison.

Treason, which is generally defined as betraying one's country, is a pretty tough item to sell, particularly because the punishment for it is unforgiving. In the United States, when Ethel and Julius Rosenberg were convicted of conspiring to share U.S. atomic secrets with the Soviet Union in the 1950s, they were executed in the electric chair. Punishments for treason throughout the world have also included being hanged, beheaded, burned at the stake, or, more commonly today, life imprisonment. Committing treason is a massive risk that comes with huge consequences, but intelligence officers are specifically trained to get people to take that risk—and to let them think it was *their idea* to do so. Intelligence officers are trained to:

> Be sufficiently confident to get a person to fulfill any request, no matter how odd or crazy it might be, within an incredibly short amount of time.
> Become viewed as a confidant—someone everyone wants to confide in, who is trusted with people's secrets, concerns, and even their darkest fears.
> Mirror the behavior of others subtly, to create an appearance of having common interests with targets.
> Exude empathy and genuinely care for their targets. Empathy is a big key to success.
> Analyze large amounts of information to get clues about what can help or hurt a mission.
> Practice discipline at the highest level. Intelligence officers are methodical, dedicated, and committed, and they work hard to remain in top physical condition.
> Be flexible and collaborative. Things go wrong all the time, but that cannot allow a mission to fall apart.

What I'm about to teach you in this book can change the way you sell your product to others—be it a brand, a business, or an idea. If there's one trait that differentiates spies from "average people," it's our ability to *confidently* act, react, and adapt. Until now, my books have been focused on various tactics that can keep you and your family safe; and while I will always be committed to sharing information about personal safety and survival, I've realized that my professional training has supplied me with additional benefits that can be put to great use in the business world or to improve everyday life.

Let me assure you: This isn't another run-of-the-mill self-help book about boosting confidence and becoming more successful as a result. There have been a million books written about that, and I'm not going to add another to the hefty pile. In this book I'm going to teach you about the ultra-secret weapon every intelligence officer carries in their arsenal: the operative mind-set. When you are trained as an intelligence officer, you are learning much more than how to defend yourself or shoot a gun at a bad guy. Being a good intelligence officer who is prepared to defend the citizens of the United States against enemies who wish the nation harm isn't just about physical survival, it's also about something much more subtle and complex. The operative mind-set includes that elusive and appealing combination of traits—likability, empathy, confidence, and intelligence—that enable a person to effortlessly succeed at anything. Another way to look at the operative mind-set? It's ultimately really good *salesmanship*.

When I began my training as an intelligence officer, I never imagined that a few years down the road the skills I would acquire in the CIA would put me in the ideal position to thrive as an entrepreneur. But in 2010, after seven years of working for the agency, I was ready to move on. I wanted to build something from scratch and work on my own terms, and I envisioned a company where I would share safety and survival tactics with everyone from stay-at-home moms and college students to high-net-worth individuals and celebrities. At the time, even my own father thought I was crazy. He couldn't believe I would leave such a steady job, especially after all the crazy hoops I had jumped through to get accepted into the CIA in the first place. It was a big change, and I was taking a major risk, especially considering only 20 percent of new businesses survive past their first year of operation. I'll admit it, I was scared.

Fast-forward just nine years later, and I'm proud to say I'm the owner of a very successful, multimillion-dollar business, Spy Escape & Evasion, that I created (with the help of my wife and some incredible team members, of course). It turns out those very skills I learned in my training as an intelligence officer had prepared me for the challenges of building, running, and growing a small business. In this book, I'm going to show you exactly how I used the operative mind-set to build the business I run today.

I'll be the first person to admit I'm an introvert—I'm a quiet guy who worked as a police officer in Virginia and eventually as a CIA officer—and no one was more surprised than I was when I won a deal on ABC's hit show *Shark Tank*, or when I landed a regular guest spot alongside Rachael Ray or Harry Connick Jr. on their national television shows. Writing one book—much less three—wasn't in my plans either. Nor was a stint doing a Las Vegas stage show at a big casino. I'm incredibly grateful to have had these opportunities, and they've certainly helped me take my business to a higher level—but I would never have gotten them down without the framework of the operative mind-set.

Ultimately, this book isn't about getting on TV shows or performing in Las Vegas (unless that's what you really want to do, then go for it), but it's about utilizing the operative mind-set to scale unexpected new heights as an entrepreneur or salesperson. Maybe you want to increase the amount of business you do so that you can hire a few employees. Perhaps it's your goal to expand your business internationally. Whatever the vision for your next big step, the operative mind-set can help you get there.

My background as an intelligence officer has proven to be a most welcome secret weapon when it comes to navigating the business world, and I'm going to show you how to use these proven tactics to achieve greater and long-lasting success, no matter what business you're in.

CHAPTER 1

THE CONFIDENCE REFLEX

CLASSIFIED

EXERCISE: Collection of information from anonymous source/or sources at one or more locations

PARTICIPANT: "Tyler"

LOCATION: Classified location, Bethesda, MD., Washington, D.C.

OBJECTIVE: Subject must navigate from classified location to Washington, D.C., Metro train station to find anonymous contact. Contact will provide subject with further information pertaining to operation. Subject must connect with additional unknown contact in Washington, D.C., to collect information concerning a potential act of terrorism directed at United States citizens.

TYLER'S STORY

I was in a deep sleep when I was woken up by a loud, forceful knock at the door of my room. A quick glance at my watch told me it was 3:10 a.m. Normally, someone pounding on the door at this hour would be alarming, but I was training as a CO (case officer) for the CIA and was taking the Long Course at the Farm. The Long Course is eighteen grueling months of training that includes everything from how to solicit valuable information from a terrorist to how to elude someone who is following you. Once I completed the course (that is, *if* I completed it), I would be an expert at tradecraft. I'd be qualified to manage other agents, spot potential agents, and recruit other agents on behalf of the United States government. (When I say "agents," what I really mean is "spies.")

It wasn't uncommon to be woken up in the middle of the night for a training exercise; they liked to catch us off guard whenever possible. The CIA wants its operatives to be ready to act without warning at any time. Terrorists and other bad guys aren't going to wait until we've had a good night's sleep before they attack us, so we must always be prepared to jump into action.

I opened the door cautiously, anticipating that this could be a simulated kidnapping and that I could be grabbed forcefully and have a bag put over my head before being dragged away and kept captive for hours. Much to my relief, there was no one on the other side of the door. All I saw was a brown envelope lying on the floor. I opened it up and found a small piece of paper that read:

7450 Wisconsin, Bethesda, MD 20814, 07:12

This address sounded familiar. I grabbed my map of the D.C. area, and a quick look confirmed that it was Bethesda Station, a major hub for the Washington Metro. I wouldn't know why until I got there, but someone (*Who?*) wanted me at Bethesda Station in just a few hours.

My immediate challenge was getting there. We're taught to avoid relying on smartphones and GPS to navigate from place to place. Maps (or, even better, our own memories) are more reliable. I was currently at a classified location away from the destination, and part of this test was arriving there, on time, with very few resources. Failure was never an option, as it meant my immediate removal from the program.

I grabbed everything I could reasonably take—the cash I had on hand, a small flashlight, and a bottle of water—and ran out the door toward the highway to face my first challenge . . . and it was a big one. I had to find someone willing to drive a strange man, alone, to Bethesda in the middle of the night. But if I had learned anything at the Farm so far, it was that being convincing enough could get a person out of nearly any situation.

I saw a pair of headlights approaching from the distance. I waved, but the driver drove right by. I didn't blame him, as I would have done the exact same thing. But approximately ten minutes later I saw another car approach. It was hard to see in the dark, and the car was moving fairly quickly. But as it got closer I noted the windows were down and loud music was playing. There was a good chance the car was full of college students. I started to get excited. This could be my ticket! The vehicle started to slow down on the shoulder of the road. I had to think quickly. Right away I noticed that the guy in the passenger seat was wearing a blue cap with a big letter G, and it gave me an idea. I just hoped it worked. "Thanks for stopping. I'm really stuck. Hey, do you guys go to Georgetown? Are you headed back? I'm Class of 2014. Poly-sci. I lived in Copley Hall." The man in the passenger seat opened the window a bit more, a good sign. "No, actually we live in Kennedy."

[SPY LESSON]

You never know when you're going to need to make a quick connection with someone. Spies stay well informed so they can more easily develop rapport with a target. Staying up to date about local events and being aware of places of note—such as popular bars, restaurants, colleges, sports facilities, stores, places of worship, and even local parks—will make it much easier to connect with customers and potential contacts. To see the special business template that I use to stay well informed and on top of my A game, you can access it for free at www .SpymasterBook.com.

"I've been walking for over an hour," I continued. "I hit a deer miles back, and my car is trashed and my cell is dead."

The guy in the passenger seat said, "Do you want to use our cell to call for help?" He was no dummy, and it was crucial that I remain calm and think of a way to convince this guy to let me in his car . . . now. I didn't want to scare him off.

"That would be awesome, but I really need to be in Bethesda this a.m. I'm driving up from Virginia Beach. I have an interview with a consulting firm, and I really want this job. I just can't risk being late. I can pay for gas if I can ride with you." I showed them the cash, which proved irresistible to a group of college kids. As one of the guys in the backseat opened the door and moved over, he explained they were also driving back from Virginia Beach.

"Oh really? It's fun, isn't it?" I asked. "My buddies and I hang out at this dive bar called Mel's. It's great, definitely hit it up the next time you drive down." I thanked them, sat back, and made polite small talk for the next couple of hours. I was feeling confident I was going to make it. They dropped me off in D.C., just in time to navigate to Bethesda Station. Part two of my challenge was about to begin.

It was 7:08 a.m. in Bethesda Station. I'd made it, but I had just a few minutes to find my contact, who could be *anyone*. As it was nearly rush hour, the constant flow of commuters was making my job almost impossible. I had zero information about whom I was supposed to meet. My head, on a swivel it seemed, scanned and scanned and scanned.

I noticed a woman in a green dress reading a newspaper. She glanced at her watch a couple of times. Was it her? Or was it the young man listening to headphones on my left? I had to find my contact soon or I would forfeit the exercise.

A train pulled in. The doors opened, and a young businesswoman carrying a briefcase and a newspaper walked toward me. The moment she caught my eye was so fast I barely registered it, but my training had taught me to be open and aware of everyone around me, and I was as positive as I could be that she was giving me a signal. She placed her newspaper in the trash and walked toward the exit.

That was all I needed. I reached into the trash, casually retrieved her newspaper, and boarded the train. I sat down and opened the paper, hoping I hadn't made a mistake and missed my connection. I was careful not to frantically flip through the paper, making it obvious I was searching for something. I'd been taught to always make sure I wasn't being followed, and I didn't want to make myself a target to another recruit or, worse, an instructor ready to admonish me for not blending in. I behaved as if I was scanning the paper for interesting articles—and there it was, written on the top of page three in blue ink, the following note:

The Willard InterContinental 08:15

Off to a hotel next. I took the Red Line to the Metro Center station and walked toward the location. I noticed a man wearing a blue baseball cap walking several paces behind me, so I crossed the street to see if he would follow me. He crossed too, a sure sign he was following me and that I'd have to watch out for him. I didn't get this far to lose now.

I entered the busy lobby of the hotel, where businessmen and tourists were starting off their days and finishing off their breakfasts. Given the bustle inside, I put myself in a position where I could see as much activity in the lobby as possible. That's when I saw him, the guy from the street. In my line of work, encounters like this are never chalked up to coincidence.

[SPY LESSON]

We have a saying in the intelligence world about encountering strangers that's worth repeating here: One time is an accident, twice is coincidence, and three times is enemy action. Successful businesspeople are often the target of crimes (like kidnapping), especially if they are public figures. Get in the habit of observing individuals around you to protect your safety.

Clearly, the guy had followed me, and I needed to do something about it. When I got close enough to approach him, he smiled and reached out his hand for a handshake. It turned out not to be a handshake but a brush pass (that's when two spies who are passing each other covertly exchange an item).

Okay, I thought, if he wasn't following me to do me harm, then he must be part of the exercise. Even though he was a total stranger, I made convincing small talk with him for a couple of minutes. To any onlooker, this would appear to be a conversation between two acquaintances who had run into each other and were catching up. He patted me on the back and walked into the restaurant over to the left. Once he'd gone, I took a look at what he'd dropped in my hand: a key to a room. That explained why he'd quietly told me he "had a meeting at 9:03" before he left. It was a room number, it had to be. How much more complicated could this exercise get?

I headed to the elevator, nervous about what was next. Exhaustion from being up all night started to set in, but I couldn't let it distract me. I made my way to the room and cautiously opened the door. Just a few seconds after I had entered, the phone rang. I answered it, imagining the impossibilities expected of me. *Am I going to have to fly across the country or scale down the side of the building?* A voice asked me to give some credentials—proof that I was who I claimed to be. Once my identity had been verified to his satisfaction, I was told to walk to the front of the hotel, where a car would be waiting for me. I headed down to the lobby and walked outside. A black car pulled up and rolled down the window. I was determined to stay focused, but I was nervous about what was next. I wasn't sure how much I could take. A hand gestured for me to move closer. I cautiously approached the vehicle. A serious man in a gray suit who looked slightly familiar said, "Get in the back, you made it through this one. Good job."

I breathed a massive sigh of relief, knowing that the exercise was over. I was now prepared to handle whatever they threw at me next.

THE MAKINGS OF A GREAT SPY:
It Starts with Mental Stamina

Tyler's story might sound like something out of a movie—a fun and exciting (and admittedly stressful) exercise that some future intelligence officers might undergo during their training, but it's actually more than that. A former instructor at the Farm, whom I'll call Bernard to protect his identity, explains it best: "The exercises trainees undergo at the Farm require incredible mental stamina. The physical training is intense, but it's the ability to handle the mental aspect of the exercises that makes someone a great intelligence officer. If you can handle that, you can do just about anything."

As someone who has undergone intense training before becoming an intelligence officer, I can tell you the people who make it through to the other side are not always the people you'd expect. They aren't necessarily the strongest, fastest, fittest, or even the most brilliant. I remember a particular instance when I was in training and our instructors were trying to physically destroy us. We were doing multiple sets of push-ups, sit-ups, and burpees. It wasn't unusual for us to be pushed until we felt like we were going to throw up or die (dying would've been quicker and less dirty!). One day I looked over, and the toughest guy in the group, the one with the most bravado, was crying. He had totally lost it. I'm not necessarily proud of my reaction—and please remember that I was sleep deprived and physically wrecked—but I started laughing. I got in trouble for it, but I just couldn't believe the toughest guy was crying his eyes out. But I was about to learn one of the most important lessons of my training and my career. Just a few feet away was a small but fierce young woman who kept to herself and had always slipped under the radar. As we progressed forward through the program, I'd come to learn she was a real dark horse who turned out to be superb at conquering whatever was thrown her way. At that moment, the determination on her face was palpable. She was also calm and focused, and she made what we were doing look *easy*. I immediately stopped laughing. I needed to keep my head straight, just like the tiny woman who was pounding out push-ups and burpees one after the other.

I understood then that my perspective on the process would determine whether I made it through the program. The instructors understood how to push us to the brink—but they also knew that if any of us truly had what it takes to do intelligence work, our mental stamina would enable us to cut right through every single challenge. I would survive training because of my brain, not the size of my biceps. I had to change my *entire focus*.

From that moment on, I was open to navigating the unknown. Was I prepared to push forward no matter how great the difficulties? Did I believe with every fiber of my being that I had what it takes to succeed? Yes, yes, of course. I would take calculated risks while always remaining calm. I'd make lightning-fast choices, always thinking on my feet. I'd do whatever it took to cross the finish line, no matter how impossible it seemed. This way of thinking got me through some incredible challenges. There were many times when I doubted myself, when I just couldn't figure out the right course of action quickly enough or I legitimately didn't know what to do next. During those difficult times, I remembered the commitment I had made to myself to succeed, and I'd dig deep and engage what I had started to call the confidence reflex: that strong inner belief that I am completely capable of jumping into action or making the right decision regardless of what I'm facing.

The confidence reflex became my default mode. The qualities that made me a successful intelligence officer have also put me in the perfect position to succeed as a businessperson. One of the biggest challenges I faced with my business had the potential to also be incredibly embarrassing. I had gotten myself on the ABC television show *Shark Tank* in February of 2014. The odds were completely stacked against me. Most of the pitches on the show are for products (and the number-one category to get funded was food and beverage). How could a guy like me, who was running a spy school in Utah, begin to compete? But I never thought about backing out, even though everyone I knew could see me fail on live television. The confidence reflex gave me that extra boost of power and motivation to go through with it, and every day I'm glad I did.

I've learned that the confidence reflex is a hybrid of essential qualities. Confidence, yes, but a good intelligence officer or businessperson is also resourceful and collaborative, can utilize problem-solving skills, be creative and show empathy, and has good emotional intelligence. Harnessing these qualities, as described below will improve anyone's business significantly.

CONFIDENCE:
YOU ARE 100 PERCENT CAPABLE OF
ACCOMPLISHING ANY GOAL YOU SET

CIA officers are deeply patriotic and believe in their mission to protect the United States against outside forces who want to do the nation harm. They believe in their ability to accomplish a mission no matter what it takes. Tyler had to accept that he must conquer every aspect of his exercise, even though he wasn't aware of the end goal. Accomplishing whatever goal he was facing was his ultimate mission. There is no room for a spy to question the worth of his mission, just as in business there's no room to doubt your product or service. While salesmen and entrepreneurs certainly don't have to be willing to die for their country, they must demonstrate an undying passion and perseverance if they want their businesses to succeed.

Actions spies take that result in increased confidence:

›   They set goal, and they always know what the end game looks like.
›   They track their progress, logging daily details about their observations and actions.
›   They follow through, and they do what they set out to do. The follow-through is a key component to succeeding at any goal.
›   They don't worry about what other people think. They are confident they are following the correct course of action.
›   They respect themselves by being honest, showing integrity and working hard.
›   They take care of their bodies by exercising and practicing a healthy lifestyle.

RESOURCEFULNESS:
YOU CAN ACHIEVE ANYTHING WITH NOTHING

Tyler had to figure out how to get himself a pretty good distance away without a mode of transportation. He didn't say, "Well, they didn't give me a car. There's no way I can reach the location in time." His training taught him to find a way, *any* way, to get from point A to point B. I also was dropped into outrageous situations where resourcefulness was the key to survival. In wilderness survival training, I was dropped off nine thousand feet up in the mountains with nothing—no tent, sleeping bag, coat (no toilet paper either). I immediately built a pile of leaves and pine needles on which to sleep. I made a lean-to shelter out of sticks and bark. When it was time to go to the bathroom? A large leaf did the trick, but I had to be sure it wasn't poisonous. Resourcefulness has no limits. If you can navigate a variety of situations with minimal resources in the business world, you are automatically giving yourself an edge over your competition. When your business grows and your access to resources increases, you'll thrive—nothing will be able to stop you.

Actions spies take to become more resourceful:

› They get "off the X." That's a phrase we use in the intelligence world, which means that if you don't get off the target, you die. To be more resourceful, be proactive; don't wait around for a solution.
› They remind themselves that they've successfully navigated difficult situations before and know they can rely on their wealth of experience to get them out of any situation.

› They aren't afraid to try new things. Spies never stop learning and are constantly adding to their arsenal of information. Push yourself to grow by trying one new thing every month.

› They don't always follow the rules perfectly. Obviously, there is a code of conduct in intelligence work, but sometimes getting things done or staying alive requires bending the rules a bit.

COLLABORATION:
SOME THINGS CAN ONLY BE ACHIEVED
WITH THE HELP OF OTHERS

Tyler could not have walked to D.C. in the amount of time he was allotted. That would have been impossible. He knew the key to overcoming his first big obstacle was to find an individual to help him. Had Tyler refused to collaborate and utilize someone else's resources, he wouldn't have made it to his location. In the intelligence world, it's important to recognize moments when help is needed and be ready to engage with another person. In my old line of work there were times when not doing so would result in someone getting killed. For instance, during one operation, the United States had the unique opportunity to work with a DIP (defector in place) who had access to real-time strategic intelligence. When planning operations like this there is a "mad minute," when issues of security, safety, health, and emergency abort are tackled in the beginning of the meeting. A very specific plan for relaying clandestine communications was created. But unfortunately, our DIP didn't follow the plan perfectly, and he waited too long to relay crucial information about his safety. He did not ask for help until his family had been forcibly removed from their home. While we were making plans to remove him immediately, we received word that he had been shot dead in the street. I'm glad to say that in my current line of work, I am not facing such dire circumstances, but I'll never forget the lesson that asking for help in a timely fashion can put you in position to succeed.

Believe it or not, I had the unusual opportunity to do a limited-engagement spy stage show on the Las Vegas Strip. I knew nothing about show business and had never set foot on a stage in my life. I knew my limits and knew that without the right help I would fail, so I had the sense to immediately seek out someone with expertise in this area. I teamed up with an experienced pro who had worked with everyone from Jennifer Lopez to the best Michael Jackson impersonator. The show wouldn't have been a success without his knowledge and expertise. Highly successful businesspeople are capable of recognizing strengths and weaknesses within themselves and their team members and can collaborate accordingly to achieve the best result.

Actions spies take to work collaboratively:

›   They set expectations. They let everyone involved
    know what the ultimate goal is and what it takes to
    get there.
›   They establish clear pathways of communication.
    In the spy world this could mean setting up clear
    signals with an asset, such as leaving chalk marks on
    a certain park bench when you want to have a meeting
    at a prearranged location. Or leaving "dead drops"

or secret notes hidden within predetermined objects such as beer cans or fake rocks for other spies. And while not as exciting, it also means filing reports and paperwork in a timely fashion.

› They recognize that other individuals may have greater expertise in certain areas than they do. Part of this is simply being open to meeting new employees or members of an organization. Open your mind to new ideas and ways of thinking.

› They treat team members with mutual respect.

PROBLEM-SOLVING SKILLS: PROBLEMS ARE NOT FEARED, THEY ARE HANDLED

Tyler's training had prepared him for the fact that problems are a part of any mission—and that's problems *plural*. There is no such thing as a flawless mission (at least not that I know of). This isn't about being negative and approaching a situation assuming that bad things are going to be thrown your way; this is about accepting that problems arise and must be solved as part of any endeavor. Tyler accepted he would encounter a series of challenges, and because his mind-set prepared him for this he was able to handle each one as it presented itself. Intelligence training teaches us that during a mission you have backups for the backups. You never bring just one flashlight; you bring a spare with plenty of batteries. You don't go out into the street with one knife; you have several. There isn't just one escape plan; there are multiple plans that consider a variety of mishaps. It's the same in business: You have multiple backups for everything from your hard drive to your email list.

Problems occur when we least expect them—natural potholes in the road of life.

Actions spies take to solve problems:

> They are aware of the various short-term and long-term obstacles they are facing.
> They remain open-minded about possible solutions, and they understand that a solution can come from anywhere.

Spies back into a solution if needed. They'll envision a positive outcome and examine the required steps needed to get there. If the goal is to extract information from a well-known scientist, a spy will home in on that individual and plan each event that needs to occur to reach that person.

They don't overanalyze. Over analysis can result in not taking action at all. A buddy of mine writes his top-secret information on water-soluble paper and hides it in the lining of a thermos. He fills the thermos with 7 Up and an Alka-Seltzer tablet. If he thinks someone is following him, he can simply toss the thermos, which explodes, and the liquid destroys the water-soluble paper. One night he was walking home and saw two guys behind him. Even though he wasn't sure if they were following him, he dropped the thermos, rendering his notes useless. Turns out they were just two guys going about their business, but my buddy knew the consequences of being wrong were dire. The bottom line? If you hesitate, you die.

CREATIVITY:
THERE ARE MANY WAYS TO APPROACH
DIFFERENT SITUATIONS

Creativity might sound like a strange quality for a spy, but if you've ever been tasked with a situation like Tyler's need for a ride on a quiet road in the middle of the night from a complete stranger, you know how important creativity is. Tyler was able to quickly convince the guys in the car that they should give him a ride because they'd all gone to the same school and he didn't want to miss out on a job interview. That was a creative story that he pulled out of thin air. Spies often have to lean on their creativity to pull off successful missions. This could entail anything from building a perfect, bulletproof cover identity to making an improvised weapon out of a soda can. Creativity can save your life. We've all heard the cliché about "thinking outside the box" at one time or another, but intelligence officers are always one big step outside of that box. They can't let their approach to the craft become routine or predictable. Encouraging creativity will keep you ahead of the game.

Actions spies take to be creative:

> Spies work on their tradecraft. They practice brush passes, map out surveillance detection routes, and even keep disguises on hand. Inevitably, by practicing your craft (whatever it may be), you'll stumble upon new approaches and obvious but overlooked ideas.
> They make connections between seemingly unrelated things. Spies are always looking for a greater meaning. If a spy is in a restaurant and sees a man talking to

a waitress, then sees another man come out of the bathroom and walk past them, the spy knows that there could be more to that encounter than meets the eye. A brush pass could have just occurred, meaning one person passed an object directly to the other without anyone taking note.

›   They aren't afraid to take risks. There aren't many "wrong" answers in creative thinking.

›   They ignore any negative voices telling them an idea is stupid.

EMPATHY:
MAKE AN EFFORT TO UNDERSTAND
WHAT OTHER PEOPLE ARE FEELING

Tyler's empathy is what enabled him to quickly assess that those kids in the car would be afraid, and rightly so, to pick up a stranger in the middle of the night. Empathy allowed Tyler to adjust his story in a way that would make the guys in the car feel comfortable enough to let him in. If Tyler had focused solely on the outcome of his mission and acted pushy and force-ful, they would have been too anxious to let him into the car. Tyler also exuded empathy when he created small talk around the topic of local bars. He wanted everyone in the car to feel safe and comfortable. Making people feel at ease in a variety of situations can lead directly to a mission's success. Spies are concerned with empathy since they are charged with getting foreigners to commit treason; it's a crucial component to their craft.

My colleague Bernard cites empathy as the number-one trait he looks for in a good intelligence officer. "An intelligence officer's job is to complete the requirement they're given, and that will often involve gathering intelligence from a source. You simply can't pull information from a source if they don't trust you, don't like you, and don't want to be around you. Subjects are well aware when they are being used, and if you're not genuine in your interactions with a subject, you will not succeed in getting the information you need."

Actions spies take to be empathetic:

› They practice seeing things from a different point of view.
› They refrain from judging.
› They are active listeners.
› They ask questions.
› They pay full attention to others.
› They focus on the well-being of others.

EMOTIONAL INTELLIGENCE: YOU CONTROL YOUR EMOTIONS AND AREN'T OVERLY IMPACTED BY THE EMOTIONS OF OTHERS

Tyler acted like a perfect spy in training throughout every stage of his exercise. Sure, at times he expressed concern that he'd made a mistake—but he acknowledged those feelings and moved forward. He didn't let doubts or anxiety take over and overpower his decision making. In other words, even though the challenge was frightening and frustrating for him, he was able to keep his emotions in check and he did not panic. While it's great to have a natural business acumen, psychologists now commonly believe that being an expert in human behavior is actually more important to a person's success. Having a good grasp of emotional intelligence is key. If you can't control your feelings, collaborate with other people, or empathize, you're not going to succeed. Rodney, a colleague of mine who has been on missions all over the world, equates emotional intelligence with his success in the field. "A big part of it is knowing how to handle criticism. Can you take criticism and process something helpful from it? Can you also listen to criticism, but allow yourself to stick to your original plan or idea because deep down you know your way is the right way? Survival often depends on being open to criticism while also knowing when to be immune to it."

Actions spies take to be emotionally intelligent:

> They are aware of their own emotions.
> They observe and are aware of their own behaviors.
> They self-reflect about why they exhibit certain emotions and behavior.
> They respond to criticism appropriately.

THE MOST SUCCESSFUL BUSINESSPEOPLE IN THE WORLD HAVE MASTERED THE CONFIDENCE REFLEX

The confidence reflex has gotten me through some of the most challenging weeks of my life. I've often wondered if I would have gotten through training without it. And while I didn't know it at the time, it turns out I was putting myself in the perfect position to succeed in the business world. My company provides protection services for A list celebrities and politicians. My Spy Escape & Evasion newsletter has over 189,000 readers, and over 37,000 people are paid subscribers on our elite membership site. (Visit www.SharpshooterU.com for a free 14-day trial of our membership.)

Now that I have my own company focusing on survival and safety, I encounter former intelligence officers who have been tasked with unimaginable situations—from capturing a known drug lord to gathering intelligence in a hostile country. My work also brings me into contact with highly successful businesspeople who have risen to the top of their fields, some of them becoming household names. It has become apparent to me that the qualities that make it possible for an intelligence officer to capture a drug lord without getting himself killed are the same qualities that enable someone to grow a business into a billion-dollar operation or run a major international corporation. Remember, I didn't have a fancy business degree or any contacts when I first started.

As I grew my business, the confidence reflex gave me a huge advantage when it came to sales and marketing, making contacts, hiring a team, and keeping a pulse on new developments and the competition. The good news for you is that you don't have to go through the rigorous training at the Farm to learn how to use the confidence reflex. Remind yourself that utilizing this reflex takes practice, and that once you seamlessly incorporate it into your work life you will experience success that you hadn't imagined possible. You can use the confidence reflex to soar to the top of any industry.

[SPY MYTHS DECODED]

ALL SPIES ARE NATURAL LINGUISTS AND ARE FLUENT IN ONE OR MORE LANGUAGES.

False!

On TV or in the movies, there is often a scene where a spy is eating at a dark table in the corner of a restaurant. He's minding his own business, enjoying his dinner, or maybe dining with a friend. The couple seated at the table next to him just happen to be carrying on a conversation in Russian. The spy will overhear a crucial piece of information about a bombing or a kidnapping they're plotting (right in the middle of a crowded restaurant), and the spy will jump up and save the day thanks to his profound ability with foreign languages. The truth is that many of us who enter training do not speak a foreign language at all (although knowing another language is obviously always a plus). Most spies will not be able to carry on a conversation in Arabic at the drop of a hat or understand a kidnapping plot in Russian. This is pure myth.

PART ONE

The SADR CYCLE, or the World's Most Effective Sales Technique

The SADR cycle, also referred to as the intelligence cycle, consists of four distinct phases: spotting, assessing, developing, and recruiting. In the spy world, it can take months or even years to plan a mission, spot and gain access to the right target, develop a relationship with that person, and ultimately "recruit" them to the cause or put them in a position to provide a spy with valuable information. This cycle is used by intelligence officers in all corners of the world. Our government uses the intelligence we gather for planning and decision-making purposes and to keep our country safe from threats such as suicide bombers or biological attacks.

If the SADR cycle is boiled down to its core components, it's ultimately the world's most effective sales technique. To get the information we need, spies sell some pretty valuable things to people who are deemed useful and well connected by the United States. These items might include freedom of religion, freedom from oppression, cash for food and housing, cash for mistresses, gifts, and expensive dinners. All of the "products" I just mentioned are commonly exchanged for a certain type of act: treason. If someone is sharing state secrets with a foreign government in exchange for any form of compensation, they're committing treason. Treason is not an easy product to sell, and that's why spies carefully utilize the four elements of the SADR cycle to close the most complicated deals in the world. For spies, it's never about meeting a quota, it's about gathering the right information from the right people to keep you and your family safe. The stakes couldn't be higher.

THE ULTIMATE SALES TOOL

What if you could gather valuable information for your business the same way the United States government does to protect its citizens? To be clear, I'm not talking about stealing insider secrets or anything illegal. I'm talking about using tools to gather information and to connect with just about any person about anything.

As anyone who runs a business knows, information is often the key to success, and the SADR cycle can be used to collect the crucial information that will allow your business to thrive or to sell any product on the planet. It doesn't matter if you're a car salesman, going door to door selling pots and pans, or the CEO of a Fortune 500 company—anyone can use these techniques to sell absolutely anything. This simple process can be used to home in on your perfect market or customer base, putting your business in a position to start earning profits *immediately*. You can quickly assess the character of a potential employee, avoiding the costly and time-consuming problems that occur when you have a bad egg on your team. You can easily keep a pulse on the competition, and you can ensure you are never blindsided by any developments that can directly impact your business. Learning to utilize the concepts in the SADR cycle is the most powerful tool you can add to your sales and business arsenal. And as I hope you'll see in these next few chapters, it can also be incredibly fun to use.

CHAPTER 2

SPOTTING

How to Quickly Identify the People Who Will Help Your Business Succeed

LOCATION: Holland, Amsterdam, Buitenveldert neighborhood. Conference Code Name: ISOKRATES

REQUIREMENT: Identify individual with knowledge and/or connection to developments pertaining to PROJECT TXT.

RYAN'S STORY

I had virtually no information to go on. I was simply told that there was a small conference taking place in Holland and that some of the best physicists in the world would be gathered there for just four days. The intelligence we had suggested that there were some significant developments being made that could impact United States security, and

I needed to find out who was responsible for them. I'd have to work more quickly than I was used to. Sometimes when you're an intelligence officer, it really feels like you're going in blind. You know *something*, but so much work needs to be done before you can get a greater understanding of the bigger picture. My years of intensive training have taught me how to look at a larger group of people and systematically home in on the ones who can provide valuable information.

I arrived at the venue, a beautiful home with a classic Dutch door painted a bright blue. The house was located on a quiet residential street in the southern part of Amsterdam. Inside were generous amounts of food and drinks, notably *bittergarnituur* and Grolsch, and the fire burning in the fireplace gave the room a nice glow. The general vibe of the gathering was sophisticated but not too stuffy. I noticed right away that the different physicists seemed to be gathered into groups. In one corner I saw a few younger-looking men and a couple of young women enjoying a conversation. They seemed to be having a good time. They were dressed slightly more casually than the other attendees. A few of the men were wearing jackets that didn't fit all that well, which signaled to me that they didn't dress up very often. I noticed one of the women tap another person in her group on the shoulder and gesture toward the fireplace. Everyone in her group turned to look in that direction, all sharing a mild look of surprise on their faces. I thought she just gave me my first clue: Whoever was gathered at the fireplace seemed to be of interest to the group. I'd make sure to keep an eye on them throughout the evening. I pretended to check my phone to buy myself a couple of minutes while I carefully considered my next step. I was curious about the group talking in front of the fireplace, as there was a constant buzz of energy taking place in that area. The size of the group remained consistently larger than others at the party—like something was pulling people to that conversation. But I would need some more time to make sure that's where my target was.

Another small group of people was gathered in the middle of the room. They were talking, and their interactions suggested they had known each other for a while. One man stood out in particular. His suit was nicely cut, not your typical college professor duds. He was engaged in the conversation, but I noticed his feet were pointed ever so slightly away from the others. For whatever reason, this guy wanted to be finished with the conversation.

I walked over toward the table where the food was laid out, at which point the man took the opportunity to approach me and open himself up to a conversation. He was in his late thirties, maybe early forties. He had on an expensive Rolex, and I could see his shoes were Italian and his tie was fine silk. This guy wasn't a professor or researcher—not with clothes like that. I turned to him, looked him in the eye, and shook his hand. "Hi, I'm Ryan." He told me his name was Clive and that he worked for a small but powerful engineering firm. His company had been mentioned in my research dossier.

I had a feeling we were both interested in the same person, which is why Clive removed himself from the group he was talking to. While I know enough to have a casual conversation about mathematics and physics, I never fool myself into thinking I can have an in-depth discussion with a true expert. I made a point of keeping the conversation casual and light—but to focus enough on Clive so that he felt important and wanted to keep talking to me. After a few minutes of chatting, I said, "Hey, so do you know those guys over there?" I pointed to the group huddled by the fireplace.

"Sure I do. Everyone here wants to talk to Thad. He's doing incredible research in the area of particle physics. Would you like to meet him?" Bingo. Not only had I identified the likely target, but I had found a way to get introduced without it seeming too forced. Clive gestured for me to follow him, and he gently broke into the group. He tapped Thad gently on the arm and said, "Meet Ryan. He's been sent here by an American consulting firm to study new developments."

Thad looked my way and said, "Nice to meet you."

I looked right into his eyes, shook his hand firmly, and said, "Well, it's really great to meet *you*."

Then he said, "This is Marcus, Francesca, Lillian, and Frank." Thad went back to his original conversation, while I chatted with the others. The evening ended a couple of hours later. I didn't get an opportunity to speak with Thad directly, but by my estimation the evening was a complete success. I went up to my room, locked the door, and began to type up my notes. I was looking forward to moving this operation into the next phase tomorrow.

I put on my overcoat and shoes and walked out of the hotel into the cool evening. It was dark and quiet on the street, and a misty air was descending on everything. I walked carefully until I entered a small but charming park a quarter mile to the north, where I sat down on a bench—the third one on the left side—and pretended to tie my shoe. It was unlikely anyone would see me sitting in the park that late at night, but I couldn't take any risks. Sitting in the park at this hour was unnatural—tying my shoelace gave me a logical reason for sitting down. I reached into my left coat pocket and pulled out a single red thumbtack. I inserted the tack into the left side of the bench. No one would ever notice it was there—except for Georgina, of course.

The tack meant one thing: "I found him. We are commencing with next steps immediately." Georgina would be so pleased when she went on her walk through the park tomorrow.

GET IN TOUCH WITH YOUR INNER ANALYST:
What's Your End Game?

Ryan's story would have started long before he arrived in Amsterdam. Analysts would have created a "requirement" based on a need by sifting through, reviewing, and evaluating information coming in from field officers all over the world. It is their job to interpret and search for patterns that might suggest certain actions that need to be taken to protect the United States. Ryan would have analyzed the requirement carefully, discussing his end goal with the analyst at length so that he knew exactly what was expected of him. Chances are, the analyst narrowed Ryan's target down from a carefully curated list of maybe ten people in the entire world who had that extremely specific ability. In the spy world, it is too time consuming and too dangerous to cast a wide net when making connections. Ryan would be deliberate about whom he met, carefully homing in on the correct individuals who could help lead him to his goal of meeting the target in his requirement.

When I started my business after leaving the CIA, I only knew a handful of people. I'm fairly introverted (contrary to what you might think and what you see in the movies, most intelligence agents are), and other than friends, family, and some acquaintances from my neighborhood and church, my network of contacts was fairly limited. I wanted to grow my business, but as an entrepreneur and a man with a family, time was my most valuable commodity, and it was scarce. I didn't see the point of going to events and spending tons of time handing out a business card to every person I met. Sure, maybe I'd get lucky and meet someone with a great connection, but that seemed like a long shot. I wanted to be efficient with my time, and I was convinced this approach would also help me reach my goals more quickly. I wanted to work smarter. My intelligence training had taught me to keep the end game in mind and set out to find people that fit into a specific criterion. Just like an analyst narrows down a list of targets, I decided to concentrate on what I most needed to make my business succeed right off the bat. Since I was starting a company in the survivalist market, I needed to align myself with people in a few particular areas. I did the market research, and I knew the demand for survival gear and supplies was there, but how would I connect with the right group of people who wanted it? How could I get involved with key players who could help leverage my business? How could I do this when thousands of others were doing the same thing?

[SPY LESSON]

THERE IS ALWAYS A WAY IN

Spies are never daunted by not immediately having the right connections. They know that no matter how far away, powerful, famous, dangerous, or reclusive a person is, there is always a way in. It's often simply a matter of figuring out which one of your contacts can bridge the gap. Spies make a habit of not just knowing their contacts . . . but knowing to whom their contacts are connected. Who do they know, who are their relatives, their neighbors, and co-workers? What unique interests do they have, and to whom are they connected as a result? But spies are also careful not to overuse their contacts, always conscious of the "give to get" concept. They'll offer favors in exchange for a warm connection or make it clear they'll be available to help out with something in the future.

Being an entrepreneur or salesperson can be very stressful and overwhelming. Thinking about how to connect and get your product in front of the right people can seem impossible. I decided to use my inner analyst to create my focus base, which consisted of the three most important categories I needed to break into for my mission of building a successful multi-seven-figure company.

MY FOCUS BASE:
What My Operation Requires to Be Successful

1. **Connections to the media:** I didn't know a single person who worked in the media, but getting on TV and radio and featuring my company in print magazines seemed essential to spreading the word about my business. I admit I wasn't thrilled about the idea of going on TV (even if I was lucky enough to figure out how to *get on* TV), but I accept that we live in a very pro-celebrity culture. Being able to say I appeared on TV or radio and wrote for magazines would give me instant credibility. That's a crucial component for a new business.

2. **Connections to affiliate groups:** Starting out, I didn't have a large customer base to market to, so connecting with affiliate groups was key. If I could strike a deal with someone with a more established brand and a larger list of customers and have them sell my product, I'd be reaching a much larger number of people than I could on my own during the infancy of my business. This would help stimulate sales and bring in revenue straight away.

3. **Connections to individuals who would do joint ventures:** Again, growing a brand new company into a seven-figure business quickly meant getting my products in front of lots of people. I needed to engage in joint ventures. I had to find other people in my industry who wanted to work together to sell a product or service to *both* our customer bases. We'd share the risk

of this venture as well as the profits. Doing a joint venture with another company that meshed well with my brand meant I was exposing a greater number of people to my products and services. This also created an opportunity for people on my list to be exposed to products they might want that I didn't sell yet. As my list grew, I realized I could also generate income from the customer base I was working hard to build by renting it out to other companies.

Once I had established my focus base, building my company into a seven-figure business suddenly seemed doable. Now I could tackle the next big step: finding individuals who could help me reach those three important base goals. Obviously, not everyone reading this book is in the survival industry, but this system works no matter what you sell. Narrowing in on the three core actions you need to take to survive results in your having a solid foundation for your business or sales practice. Remember, your focus base can be anything you like, but do some research to make sure it's on par with the expectations of your industry. As you start to home in on your focus base, spend some time thinking through these two questions:

1. **What is my end game?**

    Analysts always know what the ultimate goal is—whether it's taking out a drug lord, getting intelligence about a potential terrorist attack, or finding out which countries are making scientific developments that could be a threat to the United States. There's no room for error, since the safety of American citizens is at stake—just like the lifeblood of your business is at stake. Analysts must be purposeful and clear when creating a requirement. It's important you follow the same line of thinking when you envision your end game.

2. **What elements are key to your survival?**

Any entrepreneur will tell you that generating income is what keeps the operation afloat, and that's certainly true. But dig down one more level. What needs to happen for you to generate income as early in the process as possible? Do you need to connect to people who have decision-making authority? Purchasing authority? Do you need to connect with investors to raise capital? I knew that I couldn't wait a few years down the road to earn profits, and few of us should have to. The truth is, there's no point in starting a business only to wait patiently for years to earn a buck or two. It is important to establish a means of earning capital early on in your operation. For my business, that meant connecting with other people who had access to the audience I wanted to reach immediately. Make sure you have a clear idea of how you can make sales or generate income that isn't solely dependent on immediately having a hit product to sell to millions of people.

[SPY TIP]

SPIES NEVER STOP CASING

Casing refers to checking out and carefully observing everything that's happening around you. Spies never stop doing this—even after we retire. Casing is hardwired into us, and we are always aware of changes in our immediate environment. For example, if a new building goes up that causes a bottleneck of traffic, making it harder to leave the area in an emergency, we're going to be aware of it and investigate alternate routes. Never depend on just one route to stay safe. The same concept goes for business: Don't depend on one single avenue, as your livelihood may depend upon a different route.

THE TOP 25 HIT LIST:
SPOTTING THE PERFECT CONTACTS

We've all seen criminals on the news who make the FBI or CIA's most wanted list. These lists have included the worst criminal minds in history—from Osama Bin Laden to El Chapo. But the intelligence world doesn't just keep lists of criminals they'd like to see imprisoned for the safety of society. The intelligence world also keeps lists of the most intelligent, pioneering, and innovative individuals all over the world who have risen to the very tops of their fields. These lists could include bright minds like physicists (as in Ryan's story), mathematicians, computer programmers, hackers, and chemists. These people aren't criminals, but their knowledge is so incredibly valuable that we just don't want them to get mixed up with the wrong people. In other words, the United States prefers first dibs on whatever these people are working on, which, inevitably, gets them placed on a very different sort of "most wanted" list.

I used this exact same concept when I was ready to establish my top twenty-five hit list. I wanted to find and access the top people who could help me with my mission to develop a seven-figure or eight-figure company. Obviously, you can choose a number that's more appropriate for your line of work, but twenty-five felt right to me. It was a manageable target but one that still required me to push myself out of my comfort zone.

HOW TO DEVELOP YOUR HIT LIST

Step One: Establish Your Criteria

At this stage in the game I had no idea whom I was going to meet, but I knew I needed to develop a criterion for my hit list. I spent some time thinking about what kinds of people would be on my ultimate contact list. Again, rather than show up at every survivalist conference or event, I chose to be deliberate about my networking. The beauty of the internet is that these days it's easy to do a few searches and find out the top dogs in the industry. After all, you can see who has a huge YouTube channel, or a ton of followers on Instagram or Twitter. A simple Amazon search reveals the bestselling authors in your niche. Putting in just fifteen minutes a day on this type of social reconnaisance can create huge strides. To establish my criteria, I asked myself the following:

> What personality traits would my most wanted individuals most likely have?
> What kinds of positions would people on my hit list hold?
> What companies did I want to be connected to?

Taking the time to focus on what kinds of people I really needed to meet showed me how valuable my intelligence training really was when it came to building a business. Just like in the spy world, there are a limited number of people who meet specific requirements. Casting a wider net does not increase your chances of making good contacts (or recruiting a mathematician with a top-secret algorithm)—it just uses up valuable time.

Step Two: Identify Your Hot Zones

Spies who are sent overseas spend hours walking the streets of the city in which they are living. They get to know the culture, the danger zones, the easiest ways to get around—and, of course, where they are likely to find people who will be helpful. I wanted to follow a similar approach with my business, but I wasn't going to spend hours roaming around and taking notes. Similar to casing, I knew that systematically planning out hot zones—places where I was likely to connect with individuals I wanted to meet—would save tons of time and energy. Ryan had intelligence about a specific conference, and his sources were able to home in on a particular party. Ultimately, many intelligence officers had done the legwork to determine that the party was a good starting point, and once Ryan got there, it was clear he'd make a great connection.

I wanted my hit list to cover three specific areas: media, survivalist companies with which I could potentially partner, and high net-worth individuals who would be interested in securing my services. I would start out by casting my net broadly, eventually narrowing my options down to the best matches for me. I started seeking out my hot zones by doing the following:

> I pursued local television and radio appearances (I knew media would be a challenge, since I'd never been on TV or radio in my entire life). For my complete guide to booking TV appearances, please read the bonus section at the end of the book.
> I subscribed to magazines and other publications targeting high net-worth individuals (for example, the *Robb Report*).
> I read the latest books written by experts on the various topics I was pursuing, and I also reached out to authors. (You would be surprised how pleased an author can be to hear from someone who has read his book.)
> I paid $25,000 to join a mastermind group in which multimillion-dollar business owners hung out. At one of my very first meetings with this group, I met a guy in my industry and we put together a deal that quickly made us $250,000. If you're not in the position to make that kind of investment right now, that's fine. I also joined my local chamber of commerce, which I found very helpful. Contacting local business owners

with whom you want to connect and suggesting a
monthly meet-up is also an option.

> I pursued speaking engagements. I was able to give
speeches at large corporations, such as Rubbermaid,
to make connections and get executives to sign up
for my training. I am now very blessed to get $20,000
for a keynote speech. Again, please refer to the bonus
section for specific information about how to make
money doing speaking engagements.

Step Three: General Observation

Spies spend hours of training learning how to observe everything in their immediate environment. Initially, they'll train
their minds to notice all of the general activities in a particular area. This step is about growing accustomed to what's
happening around us. In the intelligence world we refer to the
"baseline"—we are always paying close attention to what appears "normal" or "standard" for a given situation. For example, cheering or yelling at a sporting event is normal. Sudden
silence at a baseball game may be a huge clue that something
is wrong—just as lots of shouting at church might be alarming. In Ryan's story, he would have observed the layout of the
room, including where exits and windows were located. He
would have taken note of the number of men and women in
the room. He also would have paid attention to simple things,
like how the room was laid out and how many waitresses were
working. Observing these general characteristics allowed Ryan
to determine the baseline of the room, but they also set him
up for the next very important step when spotting.

HOW TO DETERMINE THE BASELINE OF AN AREA

You may spend time in multiple environments every day. You might commute using public transportation (which could include a train station or a bus station). You have your workplace, school drop-off and pick up, shopping, or events you have to attend. Every one of those circumstances puts you in an environment with its own unique baseline. The baseline is the temperature of the area—is it loud, quiet, busy, empty, dark? For example, if you work in midtown Manhattan, the baseline is likely busy, loud, and chaotic. If you stepped out of an office building and found the street empty of cars and people, it would be a cause for concern. To establish the baseline of an area, you need to be aware of a few general things. Pay attention to the overall vibe of the room or establishment. If you're in a restaurant, it might be happy and excited (the opposite if you're at a memorial service). Note who is present. Is the place crowded or sparsely attended? What's the demographic? Last, what activities are taking place? Are people eating, chatting, reading newspapers? Who is doing what? Conditioning yourself to notice the baseline of an environment will not only keep you safer, it will help you learn to home in on individuals with whom you may want to connect.

Step Four: Observe for Relevance

General observation is really about laying the foundation for something much bigger. Observations only really matter when they are relevant to your situation. Spies are trained to observe on a deeper level—they can walk into a room, assess the situation, and determine which details matter. It could be anything from a car idling across the street, the driver clearly visible from the window; to a waitress who is pouring drinks, doing it slowly enough that she can hear every word of the conversation taking place in front of her. Why is the car there? Is the driver waiting for a signal from someone in the room? Why does the waitress want to listen in on this conversation? Is she ultimately doing something more than waiting on people? These are the kinds of details that paint the true picture, and those pictures can be very telling. The better you are at observing for relevance, the easier it will be for you to spot individuals who can help you grow your business—you'll be able to see the *real picture*.

Ryan noticed a few interesting things. He observed that the individual whom he later learned worked for an engineering firm was dressed differently from the other people in the group. His shoes and tie were expensive, suggesting he wasn't an academic like everyone else. His feet were also pointing away from the group. This signaled that he was looking for an opportunity to exit the conversation.

[SPY TIP]

FEET CAN TALK

Any time you notice someone's feet pointing away from the person to whom they are talking, it's a clear signal that they do not want to engage in the conversation any longer. The next time you're stuck talking to a dud at an event, look at your feet. It's my bet you'll notice them pointed toward the exit.

Ryan had also noticed that the group nearest the fireplace was larger than the other groups chatting in the room, and it seemed to center around one specific individual. This person seemed to be the focus of much attention, and there was activity surrounding him for a good portion of the event. This was a good indication that this person was in high demand, likely the brilliant scientist he was tasked with finding. While these details were relevant—and certainly useful—this wasn't the most notable detail that Ryan observed. When Clive volunteered to introduce Ryan to Thad, Clive gently touched Thad on the arm. For Ryan, witnessing this gesture was like winning the jackpot. It might have just been a quick physical encounter, but it had a much deeper meaning. This showed him that Clive knew Thad well enough to break into a conversation to introduce someone. It also showed that Thad was not uncomfortable being touched by Clive and wasn't reluctant to meet someone based on Clive's recommendation. In other words, the two men were in the process of establishing an alliance (I'll talk a lot about alliance building later on), and this was an ideal setup for Ryan.

Things to note:

> Who is gathered together?
> Who seems to know one another?
> Are there any people present who seem to be in great demand?
> Is there a person present who seems to know everyone?

Step Five: Cultivate the Warm Introduction

We've all been in a position where someone has reached out to us wanting specific information about our careers or the companies for which we work, whether it's to inquire about job opportunities or to just pick our brains. We want to be helpful, but sometimes this is the last thing we want to spend our time doing. It's particularly hard to say we're too busy when the request comes from a friend or relative. And while under normal circumstances many of us might not be comfortable engaging with a total stranger, we'll agree to do it in a second if the person is connected to us via someone else. Simply put, this is the warm introduction, and in the spy world it is a crucial part of many operations.

Often spies are charged with making contact with a person who is highly placed in the government, is valued for their expertise, has access to powerful people, or who, in some cases, is actually a ruthless criminal. Gaining access to people in these categories makes the job harder. That's why spies never aim to hit the source directly but to come at it from the side. It's much safer to connect with someone in the person's circle and have that individual make the introduction. As a colleague of mine says, "A warm introduction can be a game changer. You suddenly aren't a threat, you're being presented as a person who can be trusted." In Ryan's case, Clive was perfect for several reasons. He was comfortable in Thad's circle, and Thad behaved as if he trusted him. Clive was a businessperson as opposed to an academic, so he might have found becoming an acquaintance of an American like Ryan useful; thus he was more willing than the others to do a favor for him. Also, while the physical contact between Clive and Thad suggested a level of comfort, it did not demonstrate a close friendship. If Clive and Thad were tight, it's possible they would have hugged, or that Thad would have ended his current conversation to talk to him. It's also likely that Clive would be protective of his relationship with Thad, and therefore he'd be less willing to introduce him to Ryan. Clive was the ultimate warm introduction—he was able to provide access without raising any alarms at all. Subtlety is imperative, remember.

Warm introductions are the key to meeting virtually anyone you want to meet. In my experience, once I determined my focus base, I knew I needed to find people who could educate me, provide tips, and ultimately create partnerships with me. I needed to determine where I was likely to find people who had the access I needed. Thankfully, the internet makes all of this possible, so I could easily send an email to a bestselling author or to producers on the TV shows on which I wanted to appear. I could email pitches to editors at magazines for which I wanted to work. I also sent handwritten notes via FedEx: This is a great way to get the attention of CEOs and high net-worth individuals. I set up a goal for myself: I needed to contact three people a day. It might have been two calls and an email. It didn't matter as long as I was reaching out to three people every single day. As I started to make more contacts, I was able to leverage them to get other introductions.

The concept of the warm introduction was very helpful when I was trying to beef up my Facebook marketing. I had narrowed down a list of a few pros with whom I was interested in working. The only problem was that my company at the time was much smaller than the ones with which they were used to working. I needed an in so I could convince them that my company had huge potential and they should work with me even though I was just starting out. That's when I noticed that a social media marketing seminar was taking place near my home, and a little research told me that the main speaker was connected to all of the people I wanted to meet. I took the seminar and made a connection with the speaker. I had *spotted* him as a person of interest who could really help me out. I let him know how much I liked the seminar, and I thanked him for coming out to Utah. I was sure to follow up a few days later with an email saying how helpful his seminar was, and I was interested in meeting a few people who could help build my business. Could he possibly introduce me? In the end, he introduced me to the marketer with whom I ended up working. His warm introduction made all the difference.

As a person who doesn't exactly love socializing (just ask my wife), I can't imagine how I would have built my business without my intelligence training. The idea of going to a big networking party or even a business dinner doesn't exactly make me jump for joy. If you're like me and you use this process of the warm introduction, I promise you that you'll be able to connect with anyone—and without stress. You'll never dread another networking event again. For those of you who are already master networkers and conversationalists (congratulations, I envy you), rest assured that by following the practices I've outlined, you'll soon discover that you're making contacts faster, and they're more powerful and more useful to your business.

[SPY MYTHS DECODED]

SPIES ARE ALWAYS FANTASTICALLY FIT, SUAVE, AND GOOD-LOOKING, LIKE JAMES BOND.

False!

Considering that Daniel Craig, Brad Pitt, Matt Damon, and Tom Cruise have all played spies, it's safe to say that Hollywood has had a major hand in promoting the myth that spies are good-looking and sophisticated. The truth is that spies come in all shapes and sizes, and just about anyone you see on the street could be one. The scenario I've described in this chapter featured professors and researchers, who, chances are, are regular-looking people. For someone to fit in and be able to operate, they'll need to look the part, and that usually means fitting into whatever environment in which they're working. My colleagues will adapt their appearances carefully when they are out in the field. While sometimes elaborate disguises are involved, that's not what I'm talking about here. Ryan needed to blend in with a group of academics and scientists. That meant he'd likely wear a suit and tie, but nothing too flashy or expensive. If an intelligence officer is trying to fit in flawlessly at an establishment frequented by wealthy people, then he'd have a much more expensive suit, a good watch and shoes, etcetera. Ultimately, being a good spy isn't about looking like Brad Pitt, but about knowing how to dress appropriately whether you're pretending to be a college professor or a car mechanic. When it comes to intelligence work, it's true that you can't judge a book by its cover. It's what's inside that counts, and in the case of spies it's the ability to sell anything to anyone.

CHAPTER 3

ASSESSING

How to Tell Quickly If Someone Will Be Your Next Best Customer or Valued Contact

RYAN'S STORY PART 2

The last time we encountered Ryan he was in a park leaving a signal. The red thumbtack he inserted into a designated bench would indicate to his colleague that things were going as planned and it was time to take the mission to the next step. The first step in this process was simply Ryan giving off the appearance that he was just a regular attendee at the conference. That's why he was going to attend the lectures just like everyone else—and do something to make sure others saw him. It wasn't a huge conference, so it was important that he be seen and noticed by other attendees. Otherwise Ryan could have ended up raising suspicion.

June 04, 20XX, 11:30 a.m.

I was in my second lecture of the day, and I still didn't see
Thad. I was looking around the room and noting who
was there, making sure not to draw attention to myself.
I was growing a bit anxious, as the conference—aka
ISOKRATES—was only a few days long, and there was no
room for error.

The morning's schedule featured several lectures and
panel discussions on different topics, spread out over a few
buildings at the university. Unfortunately, Thad wasn't
listed as a speaker at any of them. I'd have to search him
out without making it obvious I wanted to speak to him.
I was pretty sure he was the guy I was looking for, but
I wouldn't really know if he suited the purposes of my
assignment until I had the opportunity to assess him.
Could he be motivated to help me? Could I convince him
that giving me information was something he could do?
And what motivated him? What would make it worth
it to him to take the risk of sharing this information?
Did he have the right character for our purposes? These
were important questions to which I needed answers. If
Thad didn't work out, I'd have to start from square one,
looking for someone else who might fit the criteria of my
requirement.

When the lecture was over, I started walking to the
exit when I sensed a change. I learned very quickly that
scientists are fairly reserved people, so it was clear that
something was going on. The level of chatter increased
around me, and some people seemed to be in a hurry to
pick up their belongings and get out of the room. I didn't
sense panic—I sensed excitement, similar to the buzz that

surrounded Thad during the previous night's reception. When I walked out of the lecture hall, I watched everyone else exit and walk across the street. I asked a woman who appeared to be a student where they were all going. She mentioned that it was a tradition that everyone gathered at a local restaurant for lunch. When I replied that I hadn't had much opportunity to sample the local foods, she suggested I join her and her friends. I accepted her kind offer.

When we arrived at the restaurant, everyone, including Thad, was laughing and eating and drinking. Even better, Thad was alone at the bar and not engaged in an active conversation. This was my chance. I made my way through the crowd until I was standing next to him. "Oh, hi. You're Clive's friend, right? We met yesterday, I'm Ryan." Thad stuck out his hand and I shook it. But I also took my

[SPY TIP]

CREATE AN IMPRESSION WITH A SIGNATURE HANDSHAKE

If you want to make an impression on someone immediately, shake their hand in a unique way. It's crucial you do this in a manner that's casual, confident, and easy—otherwise this could come off as strange and have the complete opposite effect. A unique handshake sends a direct signal to the other person that you're coming to them in a friendly manner. When done correctly, it's a nonthreatening demonstration of intimacy and a diplomatic win.

other hand and clasped it over both of ours. I quickly and very lightly shook his hand in both of mine, careful not to grasp his hand too hard or for too long. I only wanted him to register the fact that my handshake was unique. I didn't want to cause any alarm. His smile suggested he interpreted this gesture as I had hoped—as a minor intimacy, a sign of friendliness.

I needed to jump-start small talk, so I said, gesturing to the large crowd, "Is it always this hard to get a drink here?" Thad smirked but didn't respond further. I had to try something else. "It's really beautiful here. I've also found everyone to be very welcoming. I wish I would have brought my wife and kids."

Thad looked up, he seemed hesitant but then he said, "I don't travel very much, but I agree, it really is beautiful." His shoulders opened up, his feet turned slightly toward me, and he graced me with a genuine smile. "My family would like it too." I had an in.

"Do you have kids?" I asked him.

"I have a twelve-year-old son and a fifteen-year-old daughter. As great as it is to be at this conference, I have to admit I miss them." Thad added, "It really is hard being away from my family. I'm definitely not used to it."

Now I really felt like I was getting somewhere, so I asked, "Does your work prevent you from traveling?"

Thad looked slightly uncomfortable but said, "Well, it's very complicated for me to travel. I'm not really allowed to travel much due to the nature of my work." That sounded suspicious to me, like Thad wasn't allowed to leave his country very often. What was it about Thad's work that made it difficult for him to travel? It was another clue that I was talking to the right person.

I wanted to get more specific information from him, but I had to be extra careful about what I said next. "Wow. You must be doing some very important work if your organization can't let you go! What do you do?"

He crossed his arms over his chest, a sign of self-protection. "I'm just a researcher. I mostly work with particle physics."

Bingo. "Oh really? That's something I've always been curious about. I'd love to hear more about that sometime."

It was time to change the topic. "Do you think you'll have any opportunities to see the sites around here before you leave?" I asked. "I can't decide what I want to see the most." Thad mentioned something about a museum he had heard about, but he wasn't sure if he'd have time to go. The bartender was finally ready for our order, so I asked Thad what he was drinking. He said he had sampled a local drink yesterday and that he highly recommended it; there was nothing like it back home where he was from. I told him that it sounded great and I'd like to try it. He ordered two glasses. I quickly dropped cash on the bar to pay for them before he could even reach for his wallet. He nodded appreciatively just as a small group of students was jostling to talk to him. I thanked him for the tip and shook his hand the same way I did before, also looking him right in the eye. I walked away to talk to another group. This was the perfect time to exit the conversation, because I knew it wasn't possible to monopolize his time without others noticing.

8:30 p.m. Dinner reception

After lunch, I attended another lecture. I even asked a question at the end so that people would remember seeing me. I had carefully planned the question in advance with a little help from my team back in the States. I needed to appear like I was a legitimate attendee. When it was over, I made small talk with some others in the hallway. Then I discreetly made my way back to my room to take some notes and get dressed for dinner. I was thinking about my next move. Every conversation I had with Thad needed to be deliberate and handled with care. While I was now confident Thad held the key to the technology the United States anxiously wanted access to, I didn't know enough about his character to determine whether or not he'd be a good asset. Knowing he had a family was a start, but what else made him tick?

At the dinner table I made conversation with everyone seated there, but while others at my table were casually enjoying their meals, I was carefully observing Thad. I was assessing everyone who was present, determining whom I might want to talk to further. While assessing, I was making mental notes about who was at his table, who approached him, were any of the servers hovering around too much? A couple of times I made an excuse to get up—either to go to the men's room or get a drink. Each time I took note of the cars parked outside. I didn't see anything suspicious. But I did notice a woman get up from her table about the same time I did. I saw her walk the length of the room, positioning herself so that she could see where I was going. I'd have to watch her; it was entirely possible she'd been sent to keep tabs on Thad. When I saw her go back to her table, she seemed to focus on another man who also stood up. This was a good sign; it meant she didn't suspect me specifically.

A few speeches were made and then, finally, dessert and coffee were served in the next room. Once again, Thad was in great demand. I watched him from across the room for a few minutes, then made my way over to him. "How's it going? I just wanted to tell you that I loved that drink you recommended! I hope you'll let me buy you a drink sometime." Thad seemed pleased that I liked his recommendation.

I knew it would be a long night, because I planned to wait until all the other guests had left. I needed to get Thad to myself. Finally, as many people were going back to their rooms, I saw Thad putting on his coat. He looked tired. I approached him with an idea. "I don't know about you, but I can never sleep when I travel." He admitted he couldn't sleep either. "Hey, since we're not going to sleep anyway, let me take you out for that drink."

[SPY TIP]

GET THE FIRST MEETING

Once you've established that having a meeting with someone will be useful to you, it's crucial to set up that meeting right away, as it increases your chances for success. A spy will casually say, "Hey, what are you doing right now? Let me buy you lunch." Or "I'm free next Tuesday for dinner, I'd love to take you to your favorite restaurant." When done with confidence and just the right amount of pressure, this tactic for landing a meeting is incredibly persuasive. Remember, the object is to get the first meeting; it is not yet time to sell anything. The pitch comes later.

Thad looked doubtful, but then he said, "Sure. Why not?" I told him I had to run back to my room but that the bar in my hotel was lovely and quiet. It was the perfect place to relax and have a conversation. We agreed to meet there in fifteen minutes.

My only concern was the blond woman from dinner. She could mess up everything. I had deliberately chosen a locale that I believed would ward her off. My hotel was small, the bar was very intimate, and there was no chance she would be able to keep her presence unknown to me. Luckily, it worked. Fifteen minutes later, Thad and I were sitting in leather club chairs, discussing everything from our families, to our hopes for our children, and even our love of vintage watches. We said good night just around midnight. The evening had gone exactly how I had hoped. This subsequent in-depth conversation with Thad proved to me he was a good person and that he wasn't going to be motivated by money—it would take something much more significant to get him to share his secrets. But I thought I knew what made him tick. Thad wanted the best and brightest opportunities for his children. It would take a little more time until he fully trusted me, but I planned to make him an offer that would be extremely attractive to him and his entire family.

I needed to get on the phone with my people back in the States immediately to get the ball rolling.

THE ART OF ELICITATION

Spies are better at making conversation than just about anyone in the world. Someone like Ryan can easily have a chat with a diplomat, CEO, politician, prince, queen, or just an incredibly wealthy person. The person they're talking to might live in a castle, have his own airplane, and drive a Bentley—but it doesn't matter. Ryan could blend in well enough to appear as if he might live a similar lifestyle (and I can assure you, he doesn't). When Ryan was talking to Thad, it appeared he was just having a friendly, casual conversation. He brought up some general topics that are considered normal when you first meet someone. But something much deeper was going on than your typical getting-to-know-you chat. Ryan was actively eliciting information from Thad. A spy will have undergone literally hours of training on how to direct a conversation to pull information from someone. Every question Ryan asked Thad was deliberate. Ryan was almost like an orchestra conductor, adjusting his comments and body language to evoke particular responses. His main goal was to collect information from Thad without ever asking a direct question. Ryan was able to elicit the information he wanted without raising any suspicions and potentially scaring off the target.

Any of my colleagues will tell you that elicitation is a true art form, but Anthony was surprised by how information was elicited from him during training: "I will never forget thinking how I was above all of this in my training—that no one would get me. Then I was shown the video footage of my training, and I thought wow, that guy read me like an open book. I had to laugh. I was embarrassed, but I also realized how powerful elicitation can be when it's done well."

Elicitation works because most people generally want to be helpful and kind. It's not our nature to say no when asked a question, especially when it seems innocent enough. The truth is, most of us have used elicitation at some point in our lives. Have you ever wanted to surprise your wife with a great birthday gift, and you've asked sneaky questions to trick her into telling you what she wants? If you have, you've used elicitation. These very same kinds of tactics can be an enormous asset in the business world. When you're a salesperson or entrepreneur, it can feel like you're spending an enormous amount of time developing relationships with potential customers. Countless hours (and lots of dollars) are spent on dinners, breakfasts, and golf outings—not to mention the follow-up emails, social media posts, phone calls, and cold calls that need to be made. To make matters worse, it can be an enormous amount of time and effort only to end up back at square one: The customer doesn't place an order or the deal isn't closed. But what if, by putting some simple spy tricks into practice, you could quickly eliminate that customer who isn't going to buy from you or that contact who isn't going to be useful? What if you could pull the right information from someone to figure out if they were your next customer?

In the spy world, there is no room for wrong turns. Devoting resources toward the wrong target can derail an entire operation. That's why spies are trained in various elicitation tactics to draw information they want from a person without that person having any idea it's happening. Spies are assessing people, pulling out key bits of information to help them decide if it's beneficial to develop the relationship further. While a spy is also likely to use elicitation during the development phase, the process usually starts when he's trying to assess a potential target. He'll use a variety of techniques to get a person to start talking. Some tried and true tactics would include the following:

Flattery: It might sound cliché, but flattery can take you further than you might imagine in the spy world. Spies are expert at doling out a compliment in a manner that makes a person feel good, doesn't come off as too much—and also places them in a position to provide information. For example:

> *"Your company must really value your expertise, otherwise they wouldn't send you to this conference. You must be one of the best in the business."*

A comment like this may get someone to open up about their position at their company, share information about their area of expertise, or even talk about a project on which they are working.

Mutual Interest: If you want to find a way to get a stranger to open up to you, find a topic that matters to both of you. You'd be surprised how much information someone will willingly share once they see that you also have knowledge in this area. For example:

> *"I completely agree, the changes in home security technology are crazy right now."*

This sort of statement gives off a signal that you operate in their world too, and therefore it's safe to discuss this topic with you. You've given the impression you are knowledgeable on this topic, so the person you're eliciting feels they aren't telling you anything you don't already know.

Leading with a Question: This is a simple tactic that lays the groundwork for a more detailed discussion. It often works because many people enjoy being at the center of a conversation. For example:

> *"Have you always been with the same engineering firm?"*

This question will prompt a person to share information about their previous work history. If it turns out they've worked at the same firm for a long time, the door is now open for further questioning. What do you like about that firm? Have you ever thought of leaving?

The Ignorance Ploy: Human beings are helpful by nature and tend to enjoy providing information to someone who is asking. For example:

> *"I'm completely new to database building. What do I need to do to begin to understand all this?"*

Confessing ignorance on a topic is likely to result in someone happily educating you. Pleading ignorance often results in being given all of the information you need.

THE HOURGLASS CHAT:
How to Quickly Extract the Information You Want from Someone

If we take a closer look at Ryan's story, we'll notice something interesting. Every time Ryan got a bit of useful information out of Thad, he changed the subject. While at first glance this might appear counterintuitive, it is actually a part of a process spies use called macro to micro, or "the hourglass conversation." By starting with a broad general topic, narrowing in on a specific topic, and then going broad again, you can quickly pull incredibly valuable information from someone without them suspecting you're prying. You might ask them about their kids at the beginning of the conversation, then switch to their work (or the real information you want), then you go back to a general topic like where they like to vacation or their favorite foods. People often remember the beginning and end of a conversation—*but not the middle*. This is why spies ask the probing question in the middle of the conversation. This is how they can determine if their target has what they want without coming off as suspicious. In the business world, you can use it to assess someone's interest level in your product, what their needs are, what makes them tick, or even if they're thinking about using your competition. I share this knowledge to empower us all as businesspeople—to make useful and beneficial contacts more quickly. Just remember (and as any spy will tell you), being completely self-serving often results in a failed operation. If you want colleagues to share information with you, be prepared to give back with good intentions. With some practice, the hourglass technique is fairly easy to execute, and it can save you hours of time when it comes to prospecting new clients or customers.

Ryan needed to determine if Thad really had the level of expertise in his field that he was *believed* to have. That doesn't mean Ryan needed to personally understand Thad's work in depth, but he needed to determine if what he was working on fit the criteria. He also needed to figure out what made Thad tick and try to get a pulse on whether he was a trustworthy individual. He couldn't just blurt out, "Tell me all about your work. Is it really capable of changing the world or causing international security issues? And, given a choice, which do you prefer, money or guns?" Just as you can't say to someone you've met at an event, "Before I invest a lot of time and money into this relationship, can you just tell me how much of my product you're really going to buy?" As refreshing as that approach might be, we all know it's not socially acceptable. (It's an excellent way to lose a customer and make yourself look like a jerk.) But the same techniques Ryan used to tease the right information out of Thad can be used to feel out whether or not a potential contact is going to move forward with a deal.

HOW TO USE THE HOURGLASS TECHNIQUE

Step One: Have a Clear Objective

This technique will not help you if you have no idea what information you're looking for. Spies do their homework to have as much background information on people as possible. They're not going in cold. Arm yourself with as much information as you can before moving forward for the best results. In Ryan's case, he wanted to determine:

1. Does this person have the right expertise?
2. What motivates this person, and am I able to motivate them?
3. What's their personal character? Are they someone with whom I truly want to work?

Step Two: Micro: Deliver a Low-Key Provocative

When Ryan had the opportunity to have a direct conversation with Thad, he opened it with a low-key provocative. This is, quite simply, one-on-one small talk with the added goal of acquiring a bit of information from the person to whom you are speaking. It's very important to avoid topics that would ignite any passions, deeply held opinions, or something that might be offensive. Topics such as politics or current events should be avoided. Your goal is to find a common topic you can probe further a bit later. Ryan chose the topic of Thad's family. He delivered the following low-key provocative:

> *"It's really beautiful here. I've also found everyone to be very welcoming. I wish I would have brought my wife and kids."*

A *low-key provocative* is a statement that comes across as nonthreatening. This part of the conversation should feel easy and pleasant. Some general examples of low-key provocatives include:

> "This is my first time at this conference/event/ meeting."
> "I don't always enjoy traveling for work, but this place is fantastic."
> "It's much colder/hotter here than I expected."
> "I'm really finding the speakers here informative."
> "This seems like a very positive organization."
> "My daughter just learned how to ride a bike."
> "I bet the skiing in this area is terrific."
> "I usually walk my dog this time of night."

Assess and Observe

When he told Thad that he wished his wife could see the area, and Thad responded that *his wife* would also like it, he had successfully elicited the information that Thad was married. With a very innocuous follow-up question, Ryan also learned that Thad had children. Family was their commonality. Ryan was also careful to observe any visible physical cues. When Thad talked about his family, he exhibited positive body language, signaling that he felt comfortable and happy when talking about his family. He warmed up to this conversation by opening up physically—his feet faced toward Ryan, his chest relaxed, and he smiled. All of this information would be useful to Ryan later on as he attempted to pull more specific information from Thad.

The Four Indicators: A Place to Get Started

Of course, spies like Ryan have spent years fine-tuning their instincts. This is a skill that improves with time and practice. When you're just starting to exercise these skills in business, it might feel overwhelming. Where do you begin? How do you know what to look for? To make things easier as you're warming up to these skills, I suggest simply getting to the bottom of what someone really wants. Too often we're so busy pitching our business or services to a potential client that we never stop to think about what they're looking for or what they need. Focus on the following four areas:

Price: Can you manufacture what they're buying for less? Can you offer the same service at a discount?

Speed: Can you provide quicker service? Is your production turnaround time faster than what they are currently experiencing?

Customer Service: Are they dissatisfied with the service they're receiving? Can you provide better, faster, more reliable customer service?

Guarantees/Warranty: Do you believe in your work to the point where you can provide a fantastic guarantee? What can you offer?

Focusing in on these basic but very important areas can help you get started. If you're talking to the VP of manufacturing at a company and he mentions stress at work because their product line is behind schedule, probe for more information and see if you can solve his problem. If someone is losing clients because of inconsistent customer service, jump in and talk about how you'd handle that scenario. Like my colleagues still in the field who are digging deep to find out who might be their next biggest asset, I'm always gently pushing to see what a businessperson really wants or needs—and how I might be the one to provide it. Make a point to listen carefully and pay attention during these conversations. Notice how the other person responds physically throughout your conversation— evidence of positive body language can help you determine where you should push further or if you should back off.

Signs of positive body language might include:

› Comfortable, relaxed posture
› The individual is facing you, feet pointed toward you

> Leaning in slightly toward you
> Arms down, palms facing upward
> Using hand gestures when speaking
> Maintaining eye contact
> Head nodding the affirmative
> Laughter
> A firm but not overpowering handshake

Step Three: Micro: Narrow Down the Conversation

Once Ryan had settled on a comfortable broader topic with Thad, he could take things further by narrowing in. It was now time to ask a more direct question. Ryan pushed Thad on why he didn't travel frequently and mentioned that his work must be very important if it prevented him from traveling. Ryan was trying to get Thad to open up about where he worked and why he was prevented from traveling. It would be unusual for a person to open up widely about something so personal; if he's a valuable asset to their country and is not granted complete freedom as a result, it could even be dangerous. The idea here is to tip the domino of the conversation, to touch on it just briefly to see if it elicits a response.

Assess and Observe

When Ryan turned the subject to why he couldn't travel, Thad's physical demeanor changed again. Instead of being open and happy, he seemed uncomfortable, and his posture turned inward this time. While Ryan might not have gotten very specific information about why Thad didn't travel regularly, it was confirmed that something prevented him from doing so.

Signs of negative body language might include:

> Not making eye contact
> Looking at the ground
> Displaying an unnatural, forced smile
> Feet pointed away and toward an exit
> Tapping feet
> Checking watch
> Blinking too frequently
> Arms are crossed in front of the chest

Step Four: Macro: Broaden It Back Out

As soon as Thad showed discomfort around the topic of travel, Ryan reverted back to a broad topic. They were talking at the bar, so Ryan could effortlessly switch the conversation back to something as simple as what they would order to drink. They had a very brief conversation about local drinks, Ryan paid the bill, shook Thad's hand the same way he had the night before, and left Thad to talk to some students. The abrupt switch of conversation was deliberate, and here's why: People will generally remember the first topic of conversation they had with another person as well as the last—but everything in the middle is likely forgotten. That means that Thad was more likely to remember the warm and fuzzy conversations about his family and would associate Ryan with positive conversations. The part about travel that prompted negative feelings would be completely forgotten. Ryan would have repeated this process until he felt he was getting the appropriate information he needed to assess Thad.

CASH IS KING:
SPIES ALWAYS PICK UP THE CHECK AND PAY CASH

It's not unusual for most people these days to go for days or even weeks without touching actual money. Everyone uses debit or credit cards these days—and now it's becoming more common to pay using a smartphone. This is simply the opposite of how any intelligence officer is going to operate. To this day I pay cash whenever possible, and I'd never think of leaving the house without cash in my wallet. Spies never rely on debit cards and credit cards. Spies always carry cash, and you should too.

First, a simple twenty-dollar bill (or a few of them) can get you out of many unexpected jams. In the intelligence world, you might quickly slip a restaurant owner a few bills just to let you slip out the back door of their kitchen so you won't be detected by someone who is following you. I once was involved in a minor car accident. It wasn't my fault, but the other driver was irate and clearly not a rational person and I was in a hurry to get somewhere. He was screaming and yelling at me while my family was in the car. Two twenty-dollar bills got him quiet immediately, and we both went our separate ways.

Most important, a spy is never going to let a potential asset pick up the tab. He's also going to pay it in cash—not matter how big the bill is. You will never see a spy dropping his credit card on the table. Even in the age of technology, paying cash is a symbolic gesture. It signals to others that you are flush with money, it's no object, and, most important, it creates a dynamic where the other person feels indebted to you. Once again, this is a situation where basic human nature is a spy's best friend. Most people feel grateful when someone picks up a bill. Even if they don't have the money to reciprocate, they are likely to repay that gesture in a different form. In the spy world, this favor could be returned in the form of information or a warm connection to an important person. In the business world, such gestures also translate into a sharing of information and contacts, or they create an obligation to provide information should it be needed later on.

SPY TECHNIQUES IN ACTION:
How I Used the Hourglass Conversation to Land a Gig with a Billionaire

A few years ago, I was at an exclusive event, and I happened to know that an incredibly wealthy businessman was also going to be present. I knew that this person had been receiving death threats (this is more common with high net-worth individuals than you'd think), and I thought I was the perfect person to provide security for him. If this guy hired me to protect him or teach him some techniques to keep himself and his safer, I knew it could lead to more lucrative jobs. I couldn't just walk up to him out of the blue and announce that I was the best and he should hire me. In fact, since everyone in the room seemed desperate to talk to him, I didn't walk up to him at all. Instead, I talked to his girlfriend, who essentially acted as an access agent. I started the conversation broad, discussing the food and why we were at the event. After a few pleasantries, when I could tell she was open to speaking to me, I narrowed the conversation down to security. I told her I ran a security company, and I couldn't believe how many threats were being made against high net-worth people. The girlfriend confided in me that she was seriously worried about her boyfriend's safety. She felt that he didn't take it seriously enough, and she was looking to bring people in since he wasn't going to do it himself. After receiving this gem of information, I went broad again. I took the conversation to the topic of favorite hobbies and said it was nice meeting her but I had to go. Later on, I did make a point to reconnect with her. I called her two days later. She remembered meeting me, was glad to hear from me, and ended up hiring my company. I provided training to her billionaire boyfriend as well as his entire board of directors.

The hourglass conversation worked brilliantly. The girlfriend hired me because I made her feel comfortable around a topic that caused her anxiety. I wasn't pushy or demanding, since I knew that people were constantly trying to get her boyfriend to buy their services or invest in their company. I showed empathy and concern. A great side lesson here is that you never know who has the real hiring authority and who can get the deal done.

SPY TRAINING TAKEAWAY:
The Ability to Assess Your Own Strengths Equals Success

While it's true that a good spy can talk to almost anyone, that doesn't mean spies aren't trained to understand their own strengths and weaknesses. To survive they need to have a strong, innate awareness of areas in which they are likely to run into trouble. James, a colleague of mine who spent years working in clandestine operations (these guys go on the most secret of all missions), had to successfully perform some of the craziest exercises imaginable in order to graduate from his training program. In one particular exercise, he had to go to a local mall and, within a fairly short period of time, convince someone to give him the last four digits of their social security number or the PIN number to their ATM card. During this exercise a senior officer was monitoring him closely, so there was no chance he could get the info by (a) threatening to harm the person or (b) explaining he was in the middle of a crazy training exercise and could they just give him their PIN number? The information had to be elicited from the person using every trick in the book. James figured out fairly quickly how to get this information from someone. The ticket for him was to approach a middle-aged female cashier. He approached when there was no line and there weren't any customers around. He bought an item, making sure to share that it was for his wife. He added a few comments about how great she was and how their anniversary was coming up and he hoped she'd love it. The cashier rang up the item and told James how much it cost. It was $63.23. He said, "Really? That's so funny! Those are the last four numbers of my social! Huh, what do you think the odds of that are? You know, would you believe the only way I can remember it is to remember that my dad died when he was sixty-three and I met my wife when she was twenty-three?" More often than not, the cashier would reciprocate and share how she remembered her social security number—and he'd have the information and pass his class. James realized early on in the process that he had the greatest success eliciting this kind of information from middle-aged women. When he tried it with younger women, he flopped. Men of any age? Even worse. He didn't get anywhere. Aware of what worked best for him in that scenario, James used that knowledge to succeed and nail the exercise. He didn't have an ego about it and didn't waste his time trying to pull the same information from a thirty-year-old man.

If there's one lesson you learn early on in the spy world, it is that you can't always be everything to everyone. If you're not the kind of person who can connect easily with a drug lord you're trying to take down, you'll get killed. You put ego aside for the sake of the mission and get the right person for the job. Don't let your company miss out on a business opportunity because you aren't accessing your own strengths. Spies on TV can do anything, but the real bravery—in the intelligence world as well as in the business world—comes from knowing when someone else must take the lead.

[SPY ALERT]

What Would You Do If Someone Were Trying to Get You to Spill Your Business Secrets?

While, again, any spy will tell you that you must "give to get," you want to remain in control and share information with others only when you feel it is appropriate to do so. If someone is trying to elicit information from you, here are some instant, easy-to-use deflectors that will get the person off your back:

- Change the topic. Have a few in your back pocket. Anything will work, from cars and golf to restaurant recommendations.
- Provide a vague response if a question makes you uneasy.
- Pretend you don't know the answer to a question.
- Politely excuse yourself from the conversation.
- Draw another nearby person into the conversation.
- Have a few talking points prepared about your business that you're always willing to share. This would be the perfect time to bring them out.

CHAPTER 4

DEVELOPING

The Power of Strategic Alliances

RYAN'S STORY PART 3

Moscow, Russia, Three Months Later

By now, I knew I had something extremely enticing to offer Thad. I hoped it would be tempting enough to convince him to share information about his work with me and my team. Still, I needed to get him to trust me.

After our meeting at the conference, I made sure to keep in touch with him. We shared a few emails, and I kept the topics very general but made a point of referencing some of the things we talked about in person. I brought the conversation back to vintage watches. At the hotel, I had noticed he was wearing a watch—not anything supremely classy, like a Rolex, but it was well worn and attractive. I noticed as much about it as I could. When I shared the details with the guys from the fabrication center, they figured it was a Movado, triple date, most likely made of stainless steel. My description of it suggested it was from the 1940s. That meant the watch was either something Thad had inherited from his family or that he was drawn to well-made, vintage objects. This wasn't the kind of watch you'd pick up at your local department store. I was intrigued by it and decided to learn as much about it, and watches in general, as I could so this could be a topic of conversation—a bridge between us.

In one of our emails, I told him about a vintage Tiffany & Co. Art Deco period watch that I was thinking of buying. I had to admit, I was really starting to enjoy learning about how watches are made, especially how Thad had exposed me to something novel. I told him I was curious to know if he had something similar in his collection. He didn't, but he let me know he thought the piece would be a great one to buy. I also asked after his kids, letting him know that my oldest child was starting to think about college. I didn't bring up any topics that would raise any alarms. Any questions about work were strictly off limits. I had to assume his emails were being read by someone.

After a few months of casual emails, it was time to implement the next part of the plan. I sent Thad an email saying that I would be traveling to Moscow within the next couple of weeks for work, and could I please take him out for dinner? I explained that I didn't know a soul in his city, and I'd welcome the opportunity to dine out with a native. I made sure to add that my company was happily footing the bill. Thad responded that he'd be delighted to join me. We set a date and I told him I looked forward to seeing him soon.

Thad didn't know it, but I arrived in Moscow a few days before our scheduled meeting. I wanted to make sure my hotel room was completely secure and scope out the restaurant where we would be eating. A friend had suggested the venue because it was a classic, traditional restaurant, the kind of place a tourist would definitely want to go to, which would alleviate any suspicions. It was spacious and crowded, so it was easy to blend in. Finally, it was very expensive. Chances are Thad wouldn't have been able to afford to eat there, and I hoped the opportunity to do so would make him say yes. I even scoped out a table that I felt offered privacy without giving the impression that I was trying to stay hidden. I would slip the maître d' some cash to secure that table. Everything appeared in order.

On the night of the dinner, I was sure to arrive first. When Thad entered, I greeted him with our signature handshake. It was time for me to start developing a rapport with him. He seemed uncomfortable in the fancy setting, shifting in his seat and fidgeting. I purposely slackened my own posture to make him feel less awkward and started tapping my fingers. I asked Thad how his day was, and he shared a few tidbits about the weather and his kids. He started to relax. He was more comfortable looking me in the eye and he sat forward a bit in his seat to engage more deeply with me. I followed suit and also relaxed. I noticed that as he became more comfortable the volume of his voice increased a bit, and he spoke more slowly. Taking note of this change, I made a point of slowing down my words—just the tiniest bit. I didn't want him to notice what I was doing. We ordered our meals and continued to talk about our kids. We discussed the various challenges of raising teenagers. I was sure to throw in a few lines about how I really hoped my children would have the opportunity to attend a great university, but I worried about how expensive it would be. I made it clear that I felt education was the key to opportunities. Thad nodded, but his mannerisms changed again. I noticed that he took a deep breath, as though just thinking about his children's future was stressful. He used the word *imperative*. He said, "It is imperative that children receive a good education. I share your concerns completely."

Our food arrived, and we continued talking while we enjoyed deliciously prepared food. We talked a little about our mutual hobby, collecting old watches, but his eyes didn't seem to light up during the conversation—even when I told him about the OMEGA Speedmaster I had gotten for a steal at an estate sale (the fabrication center actually found it). It was the same style of watch that had been worn by an astronaut on a moonwalk. Since Thad didn't have a strong reaction after I mentioned the watch, I decided to try a different approach. After our plates were cleared and after we had ordered dessert, I said, "Oh! I should show you the watch!" I pulled up my sleeve, revealing a beautiful but admittedly worn watch. Before Thad could say anything, I quickly slipped off the watch and put it in his hand. I noticed a change immediately. When he felt the weight of the watch, a small smile grew on his face. He also became quiet, and he spent a few seconds observing the watch, turning it over in his hand—feeling the weight of the bracelet and running his thumb over the dial. His face changed when he held the watch; it was almost like he was in a different world for a moment.

Before he could say anything, I said, "I nearly forgot: I have a small gift for you!" I pulled out a small velvet bag from the inside of my suit jacket and handed it over to Thad. "I know you mentioned you needed a new strap for your watch. I'm not sure if this is exactly what you were looking for, but I spotted it on eBay and thought it might work."

Thad looked in the bag, leaned over, and tapped my forearm. "Yes. I can't believe it—this is perfect!"

I laughed and said, "I'm so glad, really, I'm happy to hear that. There are so many resources for watch parts in the U.S. And I'm just glad to help out a fellow collector." The truth was, that part was nearly impossible to find, and the people in fabrications back home had done an incredible job locating it, but Thad definitely didn't need to know that. Our desserts came, and we dug into the dish like we were old friends. I felt confident I was developing a rapport with Thad—we were growing closer, and I was establishing trust. I sensed he was more comfortable with me. I'd just have to keep everything moving in this direction until I knew the time was right for the big reveal. I hoped it wouldn't take too long, but I knew better than to push too hard.

BUILD ALLIANCES, NOT CONTACTS

We live in an age when any information you want, from restaurant recommendations to medical information, is a few quick
clicks away. It's incredibly easy to find information about traveling to Africa or for a great math tutor for your kid. But while
information is accessible and it's *everywhere*—many people still
let themselves get caught up in the idea of being "well connected." We don't believe human beings are as accessible as
information. It's easy to attribute someone's success to their
knowing the "right people," or traveling in the "right circles."
We might say, "Well, I'd love to work for that company—but I
don't have an *in*." Or, "My dream is to open an art gallery, but
I don't know the right people." We will spend time relentlessly
researching information about a neighborhood into which we
want to move or a new car we want to buy—we can learn every
single detail about either . . . but if there is a person in a position of power or an expert we'd like to meet, we assume it's out
of our reach.

My intelligence training has instilled in me the knowledge that, ultimately, no one is truly out of reach. There is
always a way in. What's important to understand is that
finding a way to access someone isn't the hardest part—it's
taking that relationship to a higher level that is the real challenge. There's a big difference between having a Rolodex full
of powerful names and actually being able to put the names
to good use. I would not have had the success I've had with
my company so early on if I had not made a few key connections. What made the difference for me is that I took the
time to develop rapport. I didn't just get hold of some email
addresses and start making demands and requests of people.

No one had a clue who I was. But my intelligence training had taught me how to build alliances—and an alliance isn't just a contact. An alliance is someone who views you as an asset in their own life. They trust you, are comfortable with you, respect you as a peer, and value your knowledge and expertise.

ALLIANCE BUILDING

We've all been asked simple favors from friends or family. If a good friend of yours who lives nearby asks you to check on his house while he's on vacation, chances are you'd say, "No problem. I'm happy to pop over and check things out." It's likely that this person has done favors for you in the past, and you'd be comfortable asking them to help you if you needed it. A relationship is already established, and what they are asking you to do isn't that big of a deal. If some guy at work whom you've only met once said, "Hey, I'm going on vacation. If I give you keys to my home, will you bring in my mail and check on my cat?" you'd be taken aback. You might even feel angry, like you want to avoid this person because they were so presumptuous, and the relationship is tainted before it's even begun. In the business world, people often make this mistake. They don't take the time and energy to develop rapport or build an alliance.

As entrepreneurs and salespeople, we often have to take risks, which sometimes means asking something of someone we don't know. It's never easy, and there's always a chance we can be shot down. We focus so much on *finding* the contact that we don't think through what should happen once that connection is actually made. When we find that contact, it's important to be ready to maximize the opportunity. How do we maximize the opportunity to engage with a powerful person, celebrity, or expert who can help our business? Like Ryan did with Thad, slowly but surely develop an alliance by making a connection, finding commonalities, and making the person feel comfortable. One of the main tactics an intelligence officer is going to use to start building a relationship is matching and mirroring.

MATCHING AND MIRRORING

Generally speaking, people often feel more comfortable with others who are like them. I'm not necessarily saying people like people who *look* like them (although that is often true), but most humans tend to feel more at ease with people with whom they share a commonality. Chances are you've been doing this since you were in kindergarten. If you were the kid who loved to draw, you probably sought out the kids who also liked drawing. If you were the kid who loved running around, you hung out with the kids who were playing tag. This is, very simply, human nature at work, and it's essential to think about this when you're trying to create an alliance with someone. While talking and learning to elicit the right information is crucial in espionage, spies understand that getting to know someone doesn't start with words. In fact, statistics show that only 7 percent of communication is verbal, 55 percent of our communication comes from facial expressions, and the other 38 percent comes from vocalization (pitch, tone, pauses, et cetera). To lay the foundation for a connection, spies will match and mirror the behavior of someone with whom they want to build an alliance. Learning to do this successfully will put the people you want to meet at ease and lay the groundwork for developing the relationship further.

Step One: It's Not Always about the Words

Ryan began matching and mirroring Thad's movements at the restaurant right away. He noticed that Thad seemed uncomfortable, and this caused him to move around in his seat and fidget with his hands. Ryan responded by assuming a similar posture. He wouldn't have copied Thad move for move (which would likely have been noticed and come off as strange). But he made a point of tapping his fingers, which put Thad at ease. When they started talking about their children, Thad spoke a bit more loudly and more carefully. If you want to develop a relationship, start with the movements—and let the words come later. It's very easy to underestimate how powerful bonding over movements and sounds really is. If you are a parent, you probably remember how hard it was being up in the middle of the night with a crying baby. But then one night something happened. You pick up that crying baby and suddenly she's smiling at you. At that moment, your heart melts a bit and you can almost forgive your kid for all the sleep deprivation. A smile from a baby immediately elicits a return smile from the parent (even when exhausted)—and a true connection is made. With practice, you can use this technique to start building positive alliances. There are several physical cues that people use regularly that you can match and mirror to establish a level of comfort.

> **Facial expressions:** Are they expressing anxiety, surprise, sadness, happiness? Is their expression subtle, easy to read, or exaggerated and over the top?

Posture: Are they sitting back in their chair? Or are they leaning forward? Do they hold their head in their hands, or do they sit up straight and alert?

Eye contact: Is it direct, or does this person avoid eye contact? Do they blink a lot?

Tone of voice: People naturally change their tone to express different emotions. What emotion does the tone of their voice suggest? How does it change as they move through a conversation?

Gestures: Do they talk with their hands? Do they make any specific gestures that are unique to them?

Tempo: Does their speech speed up and slow down as they talk about certain subjects?

Breathing: Does the pace of their breathing increase or decrease at times?

Physical touch and proximity: Do they tap people on the hand when they speak to emphasize a point? Or do they lean in or back as they're talking?

WHAT IF YOUR MAIN WAY TO CONNECT WITH CUSTOMERS IS OVER THE PHONE?

While you won't have access to some of the main physical cues during telephone calls, you can still definitely get a reading of someone's level of interest without seeing them in person. Tone of voice and breathing will be your main indicators. Do they sound monotone and disinterested? Is the pace of their speech picking up as they sound excited? Is the pattern of their breathing decreasing? Are they sending cues that they are trying to get off the phone (like repeating words like *um-hmm*, or *okay*)? Can you hear them doing other activities during the call, like typing? Are they tapping their fingers impatiently? These are all signs you need to either cut the call off or up your game and make the conversation more dynamic.

Once Ryan started successfully matching and mirroring Thad, Thad would have felt more at ease. Since our brains don't often easily pick up on whether someone is mirroring our behaviors, we often associate this feeling of comfort and well-being with the person to whom we are speaking. This creates the foundation of an alliance—mirroring cements the feeling that this person is a positive influence and someone we would like to have in our lives.

It's important to note that you don't have to mirror every behavior a person exhibits. You want to choose a few behaviors that feel natural and comfortable for you. If tapping your fingers on the tabletop feels totally foreign to you, it's going to come off as strange. Always attempt to keep the movements as natural as possible. The fact is, this technique can put you ahead of the game. But to do this properly, you need to make a practice of clearing your mind and fully concentrating on the conversation. This puts you in the best position to match and mirror someone appropriately.

[SPY TIP]

THE RIGHT WAY TO USE EYE CONTACT

Research shows that most people are comfortable with eye contact that lasts about 3.2 seconds. More than that can feel too intimate or even threatening. Studies also show that if the person instigating the eye contact appears trustworthy, they'll be able to hold the contact longer without causing discomfort. Always keep in mind that there are cultural differences about what is and isn't acceptable. For example, in China and Japan, eye contact isn't the norm; it's often considered offensive.

Step Two: Create a Bridge

Spies know that to successfully create a relationship with a target, they must be patient during the development process. There's no rushing things. Even though Ryan had a time crunch at the conference, he knew that if he really wanted to win Thad over he'd need to play on his terms (or let him think he was). Ryan knew that presenting the true reason behind his relationship with Thad too early would kill the entire operation. Once he had Thad feeling relatively comfortable physically, he would move on to the next phase. Ryan would start establishing bridges or commonalities with Thad. The true hallmark of a good psychological bridge is that it presents a commonality, but the person doing the developing is able to add a unique or exotic twist. For example, if you're really into hiking and another hiker tells you they've hiked the entire Pacific Crest trail alone—this puts them in a unique position. You share something in common, but that person has something additional to offer that makes them more appealing to you. This can open up another area of conversation, in which questions of interest are asked: What was that like? How did you take the time off from work? It's essentially deepening the relationship. A few examples of bridges may include:

> Having a family
> Travel experiences
> Being in the military
> Sports
> Hobbies
> Books and movies
> Music
> Place of origin
> School and education
> Conferences you've attended

With spies, knowledge is always power—and some of the biggest secrets spilled to us have started with a question as banal as "Did you go to college on the East Coast?" Make it a habit of building bridges when meeting new business contacts or potential clients—learn to be patient and let the relationship evolve. Keep in mind that a bridge *always* leads somewhere. Sure, maybe it doesn't take you exactly where you expected it to, but you need to work with wherever it takes you. For example, if you're seeking a commonality and say, "My kids have off from school next week," and the person you're talking to says, "I don't have kids," work with where that bridge has led you. Try, "Man, my buddy doesn't have kids, and I admit that I really envy his freedom sometimes. He goes on the best camping trips." That bridge just might lead you to the right place.

[SPY TIP]

LISTEN FOR KEY WORDS IN CONVERSATIONS

When you're developing a connection with someone, listen for words they use to emphasize points, or words they repeat frequently. For example, Ryan noticed that Thad used the word *imperative* when talking about college. A spy would instinctively make a point of using the same word. This is another form of mirroring that is easy to use and quickly builds rapport.

There are also a few die-hard rules that spies follow to the letter when they are developing a target. While many of these rules employ good, simple behaviors, they are crucial to getting a target or business contact to trust you, feel comfortable with you, and really open up.

> Never forget empathy, but don't confuse it with friendship. As in espionage, this is a business relationship.
> Watch one-upmanship. While you want to appear unique when creating bridges, constantly one-upping your target will backfire.
> Don't place judgment on any confessions they confide in you.
> Don't give advice unless it is specifically asked for.

> Do not interrupt or finish sentences.
> Don't change the subject of a conversation.
> Be an extraordinary listener. Show that you are interested in what they have to say.
> Use flattery, but cautiously. Don't lay it on too thick.

Take the Parallel Route

Spies also are experts at "paralleling," which is finding a common but slightly different alternative to any topic. Paralleling is about sharing a similar interest or background, though with enough differences that any obvious deficiencies in knowledge can be avoided. For example, you might love barbecuing, but your wife loves baking. Both are culinary skills, and you can have a good conversation about food preparation—but the styles are different enough that you wouldn't be expected to possess the same set of knowledge and skills. Spies like our friend Ryan are often charged with developing some of the biggest experts out there. My colleagues have solid backgrounds in areas such as mathematics, computer programming, or biology—but they never forget that someone like Thad will have knowledge that's light-years ahead of their own. They have to be careful not to engage in a conversation so advanced that the holes in their knowledge will shine through. If you're struggling to find a commonality with someone with whom you want to do business, consider the parallel route instead. If they love reading mysteries but you prefer science fiction, let the fact that you are both readers pave the way. Are you in a book group? Do you read electronically or on paper? Do you have a favorite bookstore? Paralleling can lead to engaging conversations with someone even when it seems like you have nothing in common.

> ### BORROW SOMEONE ELSE'S INTERESTS OR EXPERIENCES TO MAKE A CONNECTION
>
> Connections don't have to be limited to what we personally find interesting. If someone shares an interest that has nothing to do with you, but the topic is meaningful to your daughter, wife, or friend, then by all means bring that up. If there's a conversation about ballet and you are struggling to find a way in, consider borrowing someone else's interest: "You know, I've never personally been to the ballet, but my niece just started lessons and she's crazy about it. Maybe I should consider taking her?" When you see even the slimmest crack open up in a conversation, jump into it, even if it's not a topic that is relevant to you.

Step Three: Give to Get to Find Common Ground

When Ryan wanted to get the conversation moving with Thad, he brought up his kids. He had established early on that Thad was also a family man, so he knew this line of questioning could get him to open up further. Most of us aren't going to openly share our fears and anxieties with people we don't know, unless the other person opens or creates a warm, inviting outlet. Ryan brought up his fears about paying for his children's education, which resulted in Thad admitting he had the same hesitations. This is information that Ryan can use as he continues to develop Thad. He's uncovered a vulnerability.

Believe it or not, spies aren't always searching for someone's vulnerability to exploit it in a diabolical way—but they're going to use it to move the relationship forward in the direction they want it to go. Now that Ryan knows that Thad worries about the cost of college, he can use that to direct the conversation to other topics. Ryan might eventually ask Thad if he's ever thought of moving to the United States, so his kids could study there, for example.

While it's not especially easy to know when it's appropriate to open up to someone in a business setting, the sharing of information is almost always welcome. I'm not suggesting you drop top-secret information about your work, but any useful tidbit you share is likely to make an impact. You might not be discussing your personal concerns about the rising costs of labor (or you might, if appropriate), but sharing a way you've managed to tackle this obstacle is likely to establish you as a helpful, useful person—the kind of person with whom someone wants to form a partnership.

Make Sincerity Your Default Position

While it's true that spies are developing a rapport with someone for a very specific purpose, any of my colleagues will tell you they are connecting with that person on a sincere level. Sincerity is equally as important as making useful connections—so make it your mission to connect with others over a genuine commonality for the best results for your business. I completely agree with Warren Buffet when he said, "It takes twenty years to build a reputation and five minutes to ruin it. If you think about that, you'll do things differently." Never risk your brand or personal reputation to make a connection based on a complete falsehood—it's simply not worth it.

Learning Styles Matter Outside of the Classroom

Ryan had started building a bridge with Thad about watches, and he would have made mental notes about it, remembering as many details as he could. It's certainly possible that Ryan wasn't himself a watch collector, but this is something that piqued his interest, and he was able to sincerely pursue this commonality with Thad. He was able to use this as a bridge, but, more important, it taught him something about the way Thad processed information.

Spies are trained to notice nearly everything about human behavior—including what learning style people gravitate toward. Ryan noticed immediately that Thad wasn't very impressed by the watch when he brought it up at dinner. They had had enough conversations about timepieces for Ryan to know this watch was something Thad would be excited to see. He decided to take it off and hand it to him. Thad's demeanor changed. He felt the smooth, cool stainless steel, the heft of the bracelet, and could feel the small notches on the crown. It was at that point that Thad visibly reacted, and this suggested he was a kinesthetic learner. That meant that being able to touch something, to experience it with his own hands, was meaningful to him. It's how he processed information.

By understanding how people process information, you will be able to communicate more clearly with them, present information in a way that is attractive to them, adapt proposals in a manner that will grab their attention, and build a stronger, more meaningful relationship. The four main learning styles to look out for include:

> **Auditory learners:** If you're this kind of learner, you
> probably did well in school. People who respond to this

style like their information presented verbally, just like in the classroom. A combination of verbal instruction and body language is easiest for them to understand.

Visual learners: As the name suggests, visual learners need to be shown how something works—rather than have it just explained to them. This kind of person would appreciate pictures, diagrams, charts, and lists.

Kinesthetic learners: Just like Thad, kinesthetic learners like to touch things, to feel the materials. They benefit most from a "hands on" experience. These people may also like to move around while they're learning.

Reading and Writing learners: People who learn this way are comfortable reading and writing. They can easily absorb information from a book and understand it in their own words.

If you want to be considered a businessperson who is a great communicator, learn to utilize these different styles in your business practices. Learning to switch to different modes to meet the needs of other people will result in clearer communication, stronger connections, and, in the end, more sales.

SPY TRAINING TAKEAWAY:
How Understanding Learning Styles Landed Me Business

In 2015, a few years after my company had really gotten going, I was in talks with a large company about doing a licensing deal and I really wanted it to go through. The deal would be worth several hundred thousand dollars the first year and would soon total a number in the seven figures. This was a well-respected company, and it would be a huge boost to my business. I went in for a meeting, and the agenda was to nail down all of the final points. It was just me and one of the executives in a small room. There were some papers and books on the table, and I made sure to position myself so that these items weren't between us. I was sitting directly across from him. Since I hadn't had the opportunity to meet this person beforehand, I had to be extra prepared. I showed up at the meeting armed with everything I needed, whether he was a visual, auditory, or another type of learner. In my bag I had visuals, whiteboard markers, charts, and samples, as well as a proposal that consisted mostly of straight text. I wasn't leaving anything up for grabs. Thanks to my training, I could tell easily by his demeanor and reactions that he was a visual learner. One of the items I was hoping to partner on was a custom-made knife.

He wanted to hold and closely examine the product, turning it around in his hands. When we got to appropriate points in the conversation, I pulled out pictures and diagrams and his eyes lit up. From that moment on, I brought out visuals to support my main points and drew on the whiteboard with colored markers. I brought out my charts too. He was enthralled. In the end, I'm pleased to say, I got the deal. Even better, now that I knew this guy responded well to visual cues, I could prepare better for our meetings—and our communication has been flawless.

If you visit www.SpymasterBook.com, I put together a specific case study for you about one alliance that has made me a monumental amount of money, and how you can use it too.

SPY MYTHS DECODED

IF YOU JOIN THE CIA YOU'LL HAVE TO SAY GOODBYE TO YOUR FRIENDS AND FAMILY FOREVER.

False!

If you're wondering if Ryan was making up all the stories about his own family just to connect with Thad, he wasn't. The myth that spies have to say goodbye to friends and family is completely false, and I assure you that CIA officers still see their parents, siblings, and friends. (If you were thinking of joining the CIA to avoid having to attend your family Thanksgiving celebration ever again, I'm sorry to disappoint you.) Thousands of people work at CIA headquarters, which is almost like a mini city in itself. That means that, in addition to intelligence officers, there are security people, accountants, and people who work as administrative assistants or in human resources. There are even baristas, because the CIA has its own Starbucks.

Obviously, depending on the nature of their work, there may be some details intelligence officers can't share. It's not uncommon for an intelligence officer working out in the field to not be able to disclose their location to family members. That's not necessarily because family can't know about it, but because it's important to protect sources. However, that doesn't mean they can't be in touch with their family. There's always a way to stay connected, whether that's a special phone number or a contact at the CIA's administrative building.

UNDERSTANDING AND
ALLIANCES EQUAL SUCCESS

Once I left the CIA and started my own business, it became very clear that I view making connections differently than many other entrepreneurs. My training to dig deep, be patient, and build connections is so ingrained in me that I was barely aware I was using these tools as I was developing my business. I've said before that my personality is fairly introverted, but with these tools that hardly matters. If you can make a point of utilizing your intuition, building bridges, and viewing potential contacts as alliances—something more than just a name and email address—you'll soon find yourself making connections with people who can help you take your business to even greater heights. You might even end up with a great friend or two in the process.

CHAPTER 5

RECRUITING

Going in for the Kill and Winning Every Time

Memorandum, PROJECT Q

Date: March 26, 19XX

TO: XXXX XXXXXXXX

FROM: Ryan J. Jones

RE: Action update report regarding subject #3123 aka "Thad"

Dear Sirs:

I have been meeting regularly with "Thad" for the past three months, since our initial meeting at the ISOKRATES Conference. Our conversations, which began as cordial, have progressed to demonstrate a deeper friendship, trust, and mutual respect. To the extent that my knowledge allows, I believe Thad's skills are extraordinary, unique, and unparalleled. His involvement in PROJECT Q would be of tremendous value to the United States.

I also believe his skills and ability to conduct the necessary research are greatly hindered by limitations placed upon him by his government.

Thad is also deeply concerned for the well-being of his wife and children under the current regime. He is watched carefully—guarded, forbidden to travel—and does not wish the same future for his children. I am completely certain he will be open to our offer, which I will present in due time.

Sincerely,
Ryan J. Jones

RYAN AND THAD'S STORY PART FOUR

Thad and I had been dining together regularly and continuing our conversations. We liked talking about our kids, our hobbies, and the food we were eating. I was taking him to restaurants he could never afford on his own salary. At first my paying for the meals seemed to make him uncomfortable, but I let him know he was doing me a huge favor by keeping me company. I even invited his wife along a few times. I knew her opinion meant a great deal to him, and I wanted her to get a sense of what I was like. His wife was a poet, and I fully confessed I knew practically nothing about poetry. She enjoyed educating me, and I let her know I was fascinated by her world—even if it was something I knew so little about. She was easygoing, friendly, and very curious about my life in America. She marveled at simple stories about my travels to warm, sunny Florida in the middle of winter with my family. She admitted nothing sounded more wonderful—and she laughed as she pointed out the window, where snow was falling heavily from an all-gray sky once again.

Thad continued to open up during our visits, albeit slowly, about the restrictions he faced from his own government in his own country. This was valuable information, as I needed to keep building up an irresistible case for the offer I was going to make.

I was visiting Thad at his spartan home, where we sat by the fire drinking out of chipped teacups and trying to stay warm. It was always cold in Thad's house. I told him I had just finished reading *One Hundred Years of Solitude,* by Gabriel García Márquez, and that I found the story fascinating and the language rich and unforgettable. Had he ever read it? Thad looked at me strangely and didn't answer. "What is it?" I asked.

"I regret that we don't have much access to books here," he finally said. "There is so much great literature we are missing out on. You are truly fortunate to have opportunities to read whatever you wish." I apologized and said something about how easy it was to take such basics for granted. I grabbed my bag and started rummaging through it. "Oh! It's here!" I said, as I pulled out a tattered paperback. "Perhaps you'd like this too?" I handed over a worn copy of *To Kill a Mockingbird.* "I have no idea if this interests you, it's an American classic. I reread it once in a while, and I'm happy to leave you my copy."

Thad's eyes grew wide; the books were a much bigger gift than a lavish dinner. They represented something more important to him: freedom, access to literature, a mind-opening and intellectual experience. He said, "You really are a good friend. I'd love to read these. And what a gift that I can share these with my children!" The snow was swirling up again outside, and I announced it was time for me to walk back to my hotel. Thad embraced me in a big hug, something he had never done. I told him I'd see him for dinner next week.

A week passed, and today was the day. It had taken months of work, but I had zero doubt that my offer would be accepted. The truth is, I don't decide to make an offer to someone unless I'm 100 percent sure he's going to take it. After all, if Thad didn't accept my offer, he could go back and report it to his government; and the next time he and I met, I'd end up with a bag over my head, never to be seen again. But Thad was opening up to me both emotionally and physically—his body language suggested trust and kinship.

When Thad arrived, he looked harried. When I asked him if he was okay, he said he was, but that the walk in the cold weather had taken longer than he anticipated. He casually brushed off the snow and sat down. His spirit buoyed as he warmed up. We ordered our food, and I asked Thad about the books. He said he hadn't had a chance to read them yet, because his children had basically pounced on them—they were so excited to have something new to read. Thad admitted that it made him feel terrible that his children didn't have access to something as basic as good books. I said I was happy to hand over whatever books I had brought with me. Thad looked me in the eye and gave me a gentle squeeze on the shoulder. "You've been a good friend to me and my family. We really appreciate these gifts, more than you know." This was the moment. Everything was perfect.

I leaned forward and said quietly, "Thad, listen to me. You don't have to live like this. With the lack of freedom and the fear. I have something I've been meaning to run by you, but I'm just not sure it's something you'd be up for. I know you're very proud of the work you're doing here." Thad looked at me, intrigued. "I can help you," I said. Thad looked slightly nervous, and I had observed that when nervous he tended to rub his hands together. I mirrored this behavior, speaking more slowly and repeating a few words as if I too was anxious. I had anticipated this moment, because Thad was a deliberate, cautious guy.

"I'm, um, I'm sorry—I never should have brought it up. Never mind, please. Let's just order dessert. What I was thinking about probably isn't right for you or your family."

The suggestion of not hearing what I was going to say combined with the mention of his family was exactly what I needed to get him over the small hurdle he was facing. "No, please, tell me."

I continued confidently, looking him squarely in the eye. This immediately caused Thad to sit up straighter and prepare to listen. I explained to him how I could help his family, and to this day, the words I spoke are still classified. He was trying hard to contain his happiness, and what I had just offered was everything he had always wanted. "Thad, if you agree to come work with us, we can arrange this."

His response was exactly what I had planned for: "Yes, you know what? I think my knowledge would be very helpful to your people. Don't you agree? I could share everything I know." It was like he was selling *me* now, like all of this was his idea.

I said, "It's a one-of-a-kind opportunity. A great education, you and your wife will be free, you can read any book you want at any time!" I laughed when I mentioned the books, like this entire plan was so easy and not a big deal—he just had to go along with it.

"There is just one thing I need to tell you, Thad." I was careful to say his name repeatedly. "Thad, my employer is the United States government. We'd like you to come work for us. It may be a challenge to get you out, but rest assured we will make it happen. I am presenting the possibility of an entirely new life for you. To get the process rolling, I can give you $15,000 right now, but you have to give me something in return."

I moved my water glass from the center of the table to the side, so that he had a clear view of what I was about to do. I pulled out a piece of paper and placed it slightly to the right. I said, "I need to give the guys back home something. They need to see that you're really on board." I patted the paper lightly, indicating that it was something he needed to sign. I didn't push it toward him, not yet. I kept my hand directly on top of it at all times. "We've done it before and you and your family have nothing to worry about."

Thad was listening carefully—I knew how badly he wanted a better life for his kids. Thad reached for the paper, but I still had my hand on top of it. "Your doing this will make the world a safer place. You'll be able to use your knowledge for the pursuit of good." With that comment, I pushed the paper toward Thad. He read it quickly, signed it, and casually pushed it back to me. I put it in my bag; I had gotten what I needed. I looked at Thad and said, "This calls for a celebration. Let's order dessert."

[SPY TIP]

THE POWER OF NAME REPETITION

Dale Carnegie was right when he said, "A person's name is to him or her the sweetest and most important sound in any language." And spies know this. When you're in the process of making a deal or even if you're just networking, make a point of purposefully saying the person's name. Name repetition gets a person's attention and creates the feeling that they are interesting and the center of attention.

HOW TO REALLY MAKE AN OFFER THAT CAN'T BE REFUSED

In the classic movie *The Godfather*, Marlon Brando's character, Don Corleone, is approached by his godson for help. He desperately wants a role in a film but knows there's little chance he'll get it. Don Corleone assures his godson the part will be his and says famously of the producer, "I'm going to make him an offer he can't refuse." A short time later, the producer wakes up in bed with a severed horse head, and Corleone's godson ends up getting the part.

It's easy to think (thanks to Hollywood) that spies use force and violence to get people to do what they want. Nothing could be further from the truth. While spies are better than anyone at making offers people can't refuse, it's handled in a completely methodical manner. In the intelligence world, miscalculating the interest level of a target will instantly destroy the entire operation. Spies will get in trouble with their superiors, and they also have to worry that their target will reveal their identity to their own government, meaning the spy will soon be killed or spend the rest of their life in a foreign prison. A businessperson is not likely to be killed or tortured by someone who rejects a proposal, but when it comes to keeping a company moving in a positive direction, every deal matters. Perhaps the greatest gift to come out of my intelligence training is the knowledge of when to make the kill—knowing that exact moment when a target is ready to hear and accept my offer. I never waste time on people who end up not wanting what I have to offer. I can tell with certainty when someone is ready to make a deal, and, with practice, you'll be able to recognize it too.

THE MAGIC MOMENT

The moment a spy gets the person to accept something in exchange for information is an art form. My colleagues have spent years in the field perfecting their approach and fine-tuning their skills, and their lives depend on correctly identifying the magic moment *every single time*. Luckily you don't have to undergo years of training or live undercover in a foreign country to learn to identify the magic moment when it comes to conducting business. There are some easy-to-follow tactics to use, as well as some telltale signs that a person is getting closer to opening themselves up to your offer.

Step One: Practice Patience

Patience really is a virtue, especially in espionage. The process can't be rushed. I'm not suggesting you need to wine and dine a client for months, spending countless dollars—but you do need to invest *enough* time, until you get to know what makes them tick. What are they really like as a person? How can you make what you're selling appeal to them? As time goes on, you'll likely learn to do this more quickly, but when you're first learning to identify the magic moment don't rush yourself. The time you take will make it worth it when your offer is accepted or an order is placed for what you're selling.

Step Two: Body Language: Make a Final Assessment

Ryan was taking note of Thad's body language all along. A good spy will never stop assessing body language. They will continually note how a target responds to certain comments, actions, and outside stimuli. It's almost like a spy is putting together a case file in his mind of how a person fidgets, talks, and uses facial expressions and eye contact. As the magic moment approaches, a spy will note that the person is exhibiting receptive traits. The tells a spy has taken note of will be apparent, suggesting willingness, trust, and an eagerness to move forward. Ryan noted that Thad was making direct eye contact and had lightly tapped him on the shoulder. He knew these signs showed Thad was open and ready to receive the proposal.

> **Signs people are receptive:** They have a genuine smile (not a nervous smile), their palms are faced upwards, they're leaning in to listen to everything you're saying, they touch you lightly, their arms are displayed in an open manner.

Step Three: Ask Yourself: Are They Selling to Me?

When Thad started telling Ryan he'd be a great asset to the United States, he knew he had him. Ryan had just started dangling the carrot, but Thad knew something big was happening, and he wanted to present himself as deserving of what Ryan was going to propose—and assure him he was up for the task at hand. Whenever a client starts talking about their positive traits and why you should want to work with them, it's nearly always a sign that you've nailed the deal.

> **Signs people are selling you:** They start talking about their positive traits, they start talking about contributions they can make, they assure you of their capability, they tell you about how their skills and expertise can be useful.

Crafting the Perfect Pitch

The signs are favorable and you're 100 percent sure your subject is ready to buy what you're selling or jump on board with your proposal. It's time to go in for the kill and make your pitch. To ensure that you get someone through the magic moment to closing, you have to deliver an irresistible pitch. Ryan spent hours with Thad, getting to know him and developing rapport. He knew that the idea of freedom and access to education would mean everything to him. Someone else may have been more drawn to the idea of money or the glamour of being a spy. While other experts may tell you the perfect pitch is all in the delivery, in the spy world it's all in the personalization and presentation. To craft an award-winning pitch—one so powerful that people will be willing to leave their country of origin—take the following into consideration.

Communicate the true value: What will the person *really* get from what you're offering? My Spy Escape & Evasion classes teach everything from self-defense with improvised weapons to how to become a human lie detector. I'm ultimately selling safety and peace of mind. I offer tools that will enable people to take care of themselves and not have to depend on others for survival. When I put it this way, people want to jump on board. If I just offered "safety classes," that would sound generic and not communicate the true value of my service. We've all received a cookie-cutter pitch from a salesperson, and they fall flat every time. Craft your pitch so that the individual you're targeting understands clearly how this service will improve their lives or change the way they do business. If you want to see the full pitch for my spy training, visit www.SpySurvivalEvent.com.

Acknowledge the strongest wants or worries: Ryan knew that Thad wanted access to knowledge—Thad was an academic, after all—and he used that desire to paint a picture of how his life would improve if he accepted the offer. Parents come to me anxious about sending their children off to college, and I'm able to explain that my spy course is empowering and will put their kids in a better position to stay safe—that's alleviating a fear. The emotional benefits to buying something or engaging one's services are often huge, so develop a pitch that takes various fears and desires into consideration.

Share evidence: Ryan was essentially asking Thad to use his knowledge for the benefit of the United States. Obviously, in business the stakes can be high. But not that high. If Thad had expressed concern, Ryan would have likely shared evidence from other cases to put him at ease. Without revealing too much detail, he'd have given examples of other people in the scientific community who had gone from living a guarded life to one of complete freedom. While facts and figures are important, don't underestimate the power of an anecdotal story. Humans generally have an emotional response when they hear a story about another person in a similar situation. Providing a positive example will help push them into the magic moment.

Create a sense of community and like-mindedness: People crave connection, and we like to be associated with positive groups. When building your case, include information about the greater community—others who have benefited from your product or services. You may want to talk about your services as being part of a larger movement: For example, in the United States, Thad would be viewed as a valued academic and scientist who was respected and revered for his expertise. When I pitch my services, I might relay how empowering it will be for the company as a whole to be trained in spy skills that could save their life. Providing this service to employees makes them feel cared for by their employer, makes them feel safer overall, and provides an opportunity for employees to bond during the actual training. In the end, employees will feel like they are part of a community of positive and self-reliant individuals.

WHEN GETTING TO YES
MEANS PLAYING HARD TO GET:
Using the Takeaway Method to Vet Clients
and Make Life Easier

To be clear, I do not use my intelligence training to play games or manipulate people. This would backfire if my goal was to build a business relationship based on integrity and mutual trust. But I do believe in using the knowledge I acquired in my intelligence training to work smarter and move faster. In fact, a while back, after I had made several television appearances that boosted my sales tremendously, I realized I could coach other people about how to get on TV. Ultimately, I knew that if my approach worked for me, it could work for anyone. It turned out I got a lot of interest right away—apparently lots of people want to be on television! But while people expressed interest, I didn't want to waste my time with tire kickers; I wanted only serious clients. I realized that I could use the deliberate takeaway method to vet potential coaching clients and see who was serious about signing up. Before anyone can sign up for a coaching session, they have to fill out a questionnaire that requires a few things: They must be an entrepreneur doing at least $250,000 in business per year; they can't work in a business that deals with porn, tobacco, or alcohol; and, finally, I take only seven clients at a time and require a $100.00 deposit to reserve a phone session. Once those qualifications have been met, I send a calendar of available appointments (and I only do this coaching on Wednesday). By the time I actually speak to a client, they've been put through a number of hoops and are very excited about the prospect of working with me. To be clear, I don't do this to add an air of exclusivity to my services; I'm simply doing this to weed out people who aren't truly serious so that I save myself tons of time.

SPY TRAINING TAKEAWAY:
The Moment I Knew I Had Landed a Deal on *Shark Tank*

I'm a fairly private person, and like many people with an intelligence background, I'm also introverted. In a million years I could not have imagined that I'd go on the reality show *Shark Tank*, pitching my business on national television in front of millions of people. I knew the odds were stacked against me: that 85 percent of the people who get deals on *Shark Tank* are pushing products, and I was one of the 15 percent who was pushing a service. I knew that my Spy Escape & Evasion program had great value, but I needed to convince the Sharks it was a worthy investment.

First, I did deep, deep research. I started by reading every single book that each of the Sharks had ever written. There were quite a few and this took some time, but I wasn't going to pass up such a fantastic opportunity. Each of the people who had the power to give me a deal had written entire volumes, so this was a great way for me to learn about how each one of them approached business. I'd also hopefully be able to get a sense of their personality. After knocking off all the books on the list, I pulled every article written by a Shark or about a Shark—yet another opportunity to deepen my knowledge of each person. One of the things that caught my interest was that Daymond John seemed to have a lot of connections to people who do speaking engagements on a large scale. This is something that could really help my business. I had essentially "spotted" Daymond John. To figure out if my business might appeal to him, I'd have to "assess" him further. I eventually learned that he had a farm and several hundred acres of land, that he was outdoorsy. This was a good sign that he might be interested in my pitch.

Finally, I dug into the TV show itself. I watched every episode of *Shark Tank* and took notes on the types of questions each Shark asked. I also noted what kinds of responses pleased them, and which ones didn't. I analyzed their body language. I memorized the reactions they exhibited when they liked a product and were about to make an offer, or when they hated something and were about to bow out. Last, I watched every single TV interview that each of the Sharks had ever done. (Thank you, YouTube.)

During one interview, Daymond John casually mentioned a well-known marketer with whom he was working. I happened to know the same marketer, who, years back, had sent me a kind email. (This marketer wants to remain anonymous, which is why I'm not sharing his name.) I knew my connection to this marketer could be my key. The day before I went to do my pitch on *Shark Tank,* I printed a copy of the email. Getting dressed that morning, I folded it in half and put it in my suit pocket. I could use this information to "develop" Daymond John.

I was in "the Tank" for about fifty-five minutes. During my time there, Daymond questioned me about how I ran my business. Based on the research I had done, I knew it was time to bring out my secret weapon. I whipped the email out of my coat and said, "Daymond, I know that you know 'so and so,' and I want to read you an email he sent me." I read aloud the email, and Daymond's body language instantly changed.

This was the big shift I was looking for, and I knew I was going to get a deal. I was positive I had "recruited" Daymond

John to my cause. For the next few minutes, he began selling me about why I should partner with him. He explained what made him the best match *for me* and why our collaboration could be so fruitful. It wasn't long before he went back into "Shark mode," but it didn't matter: I knew I had him. In the end, Daymond was one of *two* Sharks who offered me a deal, and I ended up closing a deal with Daymond that gave my company an enormous boost.

MAKE THE SADR CYCLE YOUR NEW SECRET WEAPON

When used correctly, the SADR cycle can save you tons of time and cut through people who don't really want to buy your services. Practicing these tactics will help you identify your perfect customer and teach you to avoid the ones you don't want. Ryan was able to facilitate a new life with freedom for Thad. While it's easy to think of the SADR cycle as manipulative, remember that in business, the service or product you're selling is going to enhance someone's life. In the end, the SADR cycle brings people together with things they might not have known they wanted—but now that they've made the connection, they can't imagine life any other way.

While the SADR cycle is a brilliant tool that I encourage you to use, just remember that spies also know exactly when to cut bait if an asset isn't going to work. Spies won't bother moving forward with the SADR cycle if there are signs the deal isn't salvageable. If there are signs an asset isn't honest, stable, or dependable, they will stop the cycle in its tracks. If you're noticing similar signs, you should absolutely question whether it's wise to move forward. Spies also must keep momentum going at all times. Obviously, business deals hit snags and don't always move as quickly as we'd like them to, but if the momentum has come to a dead stop and you can't get it moving again, consider moving your energies to a different target.

To see a real-life case study of how I used the SADR cycle in one of my businesses that has generated millions of dollars, please visit www.SpymasterBook.com.

CHAPTER 6

THE SADR CYCLE PART FIVE, AKA (T)

How to Transfer or Terminate a Relationship for Maximum Productivity

September 25, 19XX

TO: XXXX XXXXXXXX

FROM: Ryan J. Jones

RE: Transfer plan regarding subject #3123 aka "Thad"

Dear Sirs and Madame:

Thad and his family have adjusted well to their lives in the United States. Thad's older child has proven to be nearly as brilliant as his father and will graduate from MIT next spring. Thad's work has been a positive and essential addition to keeping the United States of America secure.

I am confident of Thad's commitment and loyalty to PROJECT Q. We have developed a sincere friendship, and this mission has proven to be fruitful and positive for all involved. As I am certain of Thad's loyalty to his newly adopted home country, I am hereby informing all pertinent individuals that I will be implementing a plan to transfer Thad to his new case officer. The transfer plan will be put into effect immediately.

Sincerely,
Ryan J. Jones

THAD'S STORY PART FIVE

I was emotional as I was driving to Thad's house, most likely for the last time. Thad and his family had settled in very nicely in a small town outside of the greater Boston area. His children were thriving in school, while his wife had made friends in the community and had even started writing again. One of his sons had discovered basketball and was playing on his school team. Life was going incredibly well for them, and I was grateful to have had a hand in giving them a new chance.

My superiors were very pleased with the work I had done on this project, but I'd soon be leaving for the Middle East and I had no idea how long I'd be gone. It was time to transfer Thad.

Transferring or terminating a target is never fun, but I like to remember that the nature of my relationship with targets is unique. Targets have provided our government with services in exchange for something they want—and I have facilitated that scenario. But that doesn't mean that I don't sincerely care for the well-being of that person—I do. Thad was one of the most intelligent people I have ever met in my career, and I have had the privilege of meeting some of the brightest men and women in the world. Thad was also gracious, kind, and a great conversationalist. I always left our meetings feeling informed, like I had just had a good time with a lifelong friend. Telling him I was going to have to transfer him to a colleague wasn't something to which I was looking forward. And based on my past experiences, this process wasn't always smooth.

As I pulled up to the house on a crisp afternoon in late fall, Thad was sitting on the porch in a chair wearing a sweater. He hugged me and patted me on the back. We went inside. Unlike his home back in Russia, Thad's new home was warm and cozy. One of the first things Thad had done when he arrived was to start collecting books. He had built a large bookcase for his living room and was slowly curating an excellent library for himself. I sat on the sofa, taciturn. "What is wrong?" he asked. "You seem upset. I hope you are not unwell."

I looked up, leaned forward, and said, "I am. I have to talk to you about something today and I admit it's very hard for me."

Thad looked nervous. "Wait, you're not sending us back, are you? You promised that couldn't happen!"

I assured Thad immediately that this wasn't what I was here to discuss. "No. You never have to worry about that. I gave you my word."

Thad sighed with relief. "I'm sorry. I should never have doubted you. But please, tell me what's wrong."

"Thad, I'm moving on to another project that will take me out of the country for an extremely long time. That means I have to transfer you." Thad looked confused but didn't seem overly upset. "I won't be able to be your case officer anymore. A colleague of mine will be taking over immediately. I don't know when you'll see me again. I'm sorry, I hope you understand."

Thad sat back in his chair and rubbed his hands together. "This is disappointing, and I'm not sure what to think, but I understand. I'm always going to be grateful for what you have done for my family."

I stood up and said, "I have something for you." I pulled out a small package. Inside was a Hager watch, an American-made watch that was initially available only to CIA officers. "You're an American now. Wear this in good health." Thad smiled when he saw the gift. Since moving to the United States, his watch collection had grown significantly. "You'll be hearing from your new case officer soon. He's going to be your go-to guy from now on."

I bid goodbye to Thad and his wife and kids. As I drove down the street, I saw Thad waving in the rearview mirror. I said a silent prayer that they would all remain safe and happy here in America.

THE SADR CYCLE PART FIVE:
The (t)

By now you know that the SADR cycle has four main components, but my colleagues will be quick to tell you about part five, also known as "(t)." The "t" stands for "transfer" or "terminate." Every relationship cultivated during an operation must be wrapped up—there are no loose ends. Case officers must move on to their next mission, and decisions must be made about recruits—are they transferred or terminated? If you're wondering if "terminate" is literal and recruits are killed, you're wrong. People involved in the operation continually assess the case and determine if a recruit is still of value to the intelligence world. If he is deemed valuable, he will be transferred to another case officer. While the developing and recruiting—the most difficult part has been done—the new case officer will be charged with creating his own connection. This can be difficult when a recruit has been accustomed to his case officer. A recruit needs to feel secure and know that his new contact will manage his well-being and the safety of his family. If a recruit is no longer considered valuable, the relationship is terminated. In that case, it's almost like a breakup, but it is handled with the most delicate of kid gloves. Emotions must be managed. The asset is told the information they're giving is no longer deemed valuable for payment and that the relationship must end. Obviously, this person can get very angry and blow the officer's cover, which presents a real problem.

THE FLAWLESS TRANSFER: THE ULTIMATE EXAMPLE OF GOOD CLIENT MANAGEMENT

The stakes are highest when an individual feels neglected or even betrayed when moved to a new case officer. Because the transfer can be so difficult, it is handled very carefully. What I never anticipated from my intelligence training was that I was learning an invaluable lesson about client management.

We all know that when you're an entrepreneur or small businessperson, it's tempting to try to handle everything yourself. We want to make sure the biggest and best clients are treated with respect and feel they are getting your personal attention. Entrepreneurs also learn that if they want their business to grow they must continue expanding the company's Rolodex. The CEO or head of any company needs to think like a spy—and move forward or die. It's nearly impossible to keep building a business when personally managing all of the important client or customer relationships.

The United States has intelligence officers planted all over the world who are constantly gathering information. Yet it's often the case that businesspeople don't make a point of continually collecting information on their most important assets—their clients and customers. One of the most valuable lessons I've learned from my training is that arming yourself (and your team members) with information is the key to transferring a client or customer successfully to another team member, affording the time to grow the company to new heights. At Spy Escape & Evasion, I've created a practice where team members are carefully briefed before they take over client relationships. This is a two-part process that has kept clients happy, allowed team members to do their best work, and provided opportunities to upsell and make repeat sells to our very best customers.

Phase One: Preparing Your Team Members

Make the right match: Be deliberate about transferring a client to a new point person. Don't simply make decisions based on who on your team has the most time available to take someone on or who has the most experience. Take things a step further and consider who will click with whom, who has commonalities, or whose personality would be the best fit. If you have an incredibly high-energy team member, you'll have to consider if they are really the best match for a customer who is reserved and low-key. If you have a customer who requires patience and hand holding, think about who on your team is especially equipped to handle that.

Keep in mind that in the spy world, transfers have the greatest chance of success when there are fewer people involved in the process. Spies are all about one-on-one interactions. Obviously, this kind of ratio isn't possible to duplicate in many businesses, but there's something to be learned from it. Personal, uncomplicated relationships have the greatest chance of flourishing. At Spy Escape & Evasion, we aim to make our customers feel like they're working with a small business, and we intend to retain this feeling as our company grows larger.

Lay out all expectations in detail: It's impossible to meet expectations if you don't know what they are. That's why a spy is carefully briefed about the expectations of every aspect of a mission. What is he there to do? What kind of information would be deemed useful or valuable?

Whenever I bring on a new client and am ready to transfer him to a team member, I carefully disclose all of the expectations this person has that must be met. If I guaranteed a large order would be fulfilled in ninety days, a customer's new contact at my company needs to know that. Any discounts, promises, concerns, or potential issues need to be made available to the new point person in order for this relationship to succeed. Ultimately, strong sales result from good customer service—and that begins when expectations are clear and transparent.

We take detailed notes on what we call a client contact sheet. Such detailed notes about interactions, personal details, and any bumps or bruises that have been encountered can be invaluable for client retention.

Brief your team member on the customer. Include as many details as possible. Ryan and Thad's story shows how hard intelligence officers work in order to really get to know a target. I make a point to never stop developing a relationship with my customers. I always want to know what they want, what they feel they need, and generally what their lives are like. Obviously, a mother of four is likely to be interested in different products than a young kid who is just going to college. Just as Ryan continued to learn about Thad, I'm always trying to understand what makes a person tick. Staying up to date on how customers are doing as people is about being a good human being and placing yourself in the best position to serve them well. Just like in the intelligence world, the more information I have, the more smoothly the operation can run.

Habitually record data to provide the best customer experience: While I'm fortunate to have a fantastic team I work with and whom I trust implicitly, I make sure to keep detailed records about not just what people are buying and when, but what's actually going on with our customers. If someone has had a baby or gotten transferred to a new company, we want to know right away so we can continue to meet their needs in the best way possible. Every time an intelligence officer like Ryan met with a target, he would fill out a contact report. We use the very same system in my office. Every time contact is made between customer support and a customer, a report is filled out so that anyone in the business can access the information. Obviously, it's not our business to pry very personal information from people, but when we learn that "Thomas Smith loves golf and takes several golf outings a year," we'll note that. The next time one of us talks to Tom, we will ask how his last golf trip was. This is incredibly easy to do, and it has the effect of making clients feel like valued individuals. I've included a sample of an actual contact report tailored to fit the needs of my own business. While the information below is specific to me and my business, you can tailor it . . .

[FOR YOUR EYES ONLY]

CONTACT REPORT

DATE, PLACE & TIME OF CONTACT: 15 July 2017/20:00, Annual Survival convention

PARTICIPANTS: Lisa of Spy Escape & Evasion Team, Thomas Smith

Thomas is extremely pleased with the level of service. We included free tactical pens with his last order, which he distributed to his employees. He is interested in booking an in-company training with Jason. I also mentioned we have the Advanced Spy Course coming up in May. He is planning his big dream golf trip to Scotland for his fiftieth birthday in October.

FOLLOW-UP ACTION: Sent email 16 July 2017, including information about booking speaking engagement and Advanced Spy Course.

DATE, PLACE & TIME OF CONTACT: 29 July 2017/20:00, phone call

PARTICIPANTS: Lisa of Spy Escape & Evasion Team, Thomas Smith

Thomas booked in-company training. He has some questions about the Advanced Spy Course. Collected logistic information for training. Wished him well on his upcoming trip.

FOLLOW-UP ACTION: Sent Jason Hanson email with questions so I can provide him with most detailed answer. Set reminder to send birthday card from the company.

DATE, PLACE & TIME OF CONTACT: 12 September 2017/20:00, phone call.

PARTICIPANTS: Lisa of Spy Escape & Evasion Team, Thomas Smith

Called to see how trip was and finalize logistics for the in-company training. The golf trip went great and he's planning a Christmas golf trip to the Bahamas. Asked if he had any further questions about Advanced Spy Course. He replied he was curious about the best hotels and restaurants. I think he's close to signing up!

FOLLOW-UP ACTION: Send Thomas information regarding good hotel deals in Las Vegas. Ask Jason to send a personal email telling Thomas he'd love to see him at the Advanced Spy Course. Remind him there are only five spots left!

Phase Two:
Preparing Your Client or Customer for the Transition

When I decide to transfer a customer to one of my team members, I have no doubt that the customer will receive excellent service. Our number-one team motto is "Treat customers like family." That essentially means that while I might be taking a step back, another family member is jumping right in. I don't just stop all contact with the customer and let my team member take over. Though I have an incredibly capable team, I recognize that not preparing the client for the transition can put a strain on the relationship. That makes things difficult for both the customer and the team member. We make sure clients feel taken care of and that they're in good hands by doing the following:

Making an Introduction

Before or during transfer, I reach out to the client and let them know how much I value their business. If I've decided Lisa is their best match, I'll let them know I'm excited for them to connect with her, and I'll be sure to throw in a few tidbits about why I think Lisa will be terrific. I'll talk about how Lisa's strengths and unique qualities will be a benefit to working with her. I want it to be clear that I've made a deliberate match—I'm not just tossing the business to whomever is available. I'm also sure to connect the client with Lisa directly. Depending on the nature of your business or the size of your account, you'll need to decide if this is something that can be done over email, on the phone, or if it's best to meet in person.

Reaching Out and Checking In

I know I don't need to look over my employees' shoulders (they always go above and beyond and overdeliver), but that doesn't mean I don't touch base with big accounts from time to time. Reach out periodically to check in, and reiterate that you appreciate their business and hope they're doing well. This is an effective way to let your customers know you care about them. This is also an instance when contact reports come in incredibly handy. From the example provided above, I learned that Thomas had returned from his big golf trip to Scotland, which meant I could ask him how it went and that I had useful information with which to establish rapport. These small but sincere personal touches often get lost along the wayside, especially with so much commerce being done on the internet. Don't underestimate the impact of putting a personal, human touch on your customer service experience.

THE TERMINATION: PETER'S STORY

The following story featuring Magda and Peter demonstrates what happens when a relationship in the spy world isn't running so smoothly.

"Magda" was brilliant, but it turned out that she was also very dangerous. I spotted her at a popular tea house in a neighborhood where many researchers and professors from XXXX XXXXXX University lived. It was a well-appointed neighborhood, with beautiful old buildings

gracing every street. Magda was born in the Middle East
but was educated in America at MIT. The background
from my analyst suggested that her unique knowledge of
XXXX XXXXXXX could be essential to new developments
in biowarfare. I engaged with her after some careful
observation and began the long cycle of developing her.
I managed a warm introduction at a faculty party I had
gotten my way into and set up the first meeting. It went
well, and it was obvious she would be a fantastic asset to
the United States government. I met with her in various
cafes and restaurants throughout the city for many
months. She shared our deep concern that her knowledge
of XXXX XXXXXXX could be used to hurt innocent
people in a terrorist attack. She felt comfortable with the
idea that her information would be safer in the hands of
the United States.

We agreed to meet at a museum near her office
at a particular time, but she didn't show up. Nor did
she send one of our predetermined signals that would
indicate to me that something had come up. My first
reaction was to worry. I had carefully conducted a
surveillance detection route and I was positive I wasn't
being followed. But was Magda being as careful?
Making sure no one was watching me, I headed home
and used our signal to contact her. She answered
immediately. When I asked her where she had been,
she stuttered and made up an excuse about being busy.
I had given her a codeword, "tenure," that she could
mutter in the event she was being held against her will.
She didn't use the codeword, and it seemed that she
had genuinely forgotten or hadn't wanted to meet. This
made me ask myself whether she was truly dedicated to

our cause. I made it clear that I needed to see her the following morning and set up a time and meeting place.

When Magda arrived, she looked agitated. I asked her if she was concerned about her tenure, which was code for "is someone threatening you?" She said no, she wasn't worried. She was just busy. She drank her coffee hastily and said she had to go. My heart sank a bit. For some reason, Magda had had second thoughts about what she was doing. She wasn't fully committed, and an asset who is on the fence about what they're doing is a massive risk. I went home and then set up another meeting with Magda. I could tell by the tone of her voice that she was reluctant to meet. I told her it was of utmost importance. When she arrived, I sat back in my chair and appeared serious, which she recognized. "What's wrong?" she asked. I leaned forward and gently explained her services weren't needed anymore. Her face took on a frightened look. "Did I do something wrong?"

I looked at her and, with a sincere half-smile, said, "Magda, you have nothing to worry about. Thank you, but your services are no longer needed." I dropped cash on the table and walked out of the restaurant. I was sad to lose Magda—but an asset that isn't dedicated to the mission is simply too risky. I'd have to find a new target.

THE CUSTOMER IS NOT ALWAYS RIGHT:
Learn to Cut Losses Quickly to Save Time and Money

The second that Peter felt Magda might not be fully committed to their work together, he had no choice but to let her go. By now you know that the development process takes a long time, so the failure to recruit her would have been a huge setback. But it's impossible to risk working with an agent who isn't fully dedicated, as the risk that they will be open to manipulation by individuals from other countries or agencies is too great. That's why an asset who isn't toeing the line will be terminated immediately. There are no second chances.

I'm certainly not suggesting that there should be no second chances in the workplace (everyone makes mistakes), but I am trying to relay the importance of saving yourself precious time and energy if a client isn't being respectful and conducive to your mission. I can't tell you how many times a friend of mine has told me a story about a bad client—a guy who is abusive, yells and screams, makes outrageous demands, and can never be pleased. Then I'll hear about how people are bending over backward to make this guy happy. They'll placate him for a few days or maybe a week, and then the cycle just starts over again. In my book, the customer is *not always right*. That's the biggest myth in business. If someone is abusive to your team, difficult, and causing constant drama, they should be let go immediately. In the intelligence field, a bad egg is removed immediately, and I follow a similar creed in my own business. An uber difficult client isn't worth any amount of money. A terrible client will infect your team and their morale like a cancer.

If you look at the resources and energy this individual is sucking up, you'll see that, chances are, they're not worth it.

Time, energy, and even personal happiness are your most valuable commodities, and they should be directed toward finding new clients who exhibit acceptable behavior.

KNOW YOUR VALUES
(AND ACT ON THEM WITHOUT RESERVATION)

I remember the early days of starting my company, when I had just left a solid job at the CIA that had a regular paycheck and great benefits. All entrepreneurs know what it feels like to be building something from the ground up—it's thrilling, but it's also terrifying when you realize you don't know when your next paycheck is coming (or if it's ever going to come at all). If you let the fear of the unknown guide you in your decision-making process, you're going to make choices based on money. This approach often results in taking on a client whom you know will be difficult or letting a customer batter around your entire staff because he's "paying good money."

When you join the CIA, you take an oath. After initiation week ends and you've spent an entire week with all of the other recruits, you're taken to the CIA headquarters in Langley, Virginia. Everyone states the following:

> "I, [name], do solemnly swear (or affirm) that I will support and defend the Constitution of the United States against all enemies, foreign and domestic; that I will bear true faith and allegiance to the same; that I take this obligation freely, without any mental reservation or purpose of evasion; and that I will well and faithfully discharge the duties of the office on which I am about to enter. So help me God."

Like all of my brothers and sisters in the CIA, I took my oath very seriously. I was proud to defend the United States of America against her enemies, without any reservation whatsoever. I decided that when I started my own company, I would outline my core values and beliefs, and I would make a pact with myself and all of my team members to follow them closely. A framed copy of my company's core beliefs hangs in my office as a reminder of what I stand for. It reads:

Our mission for the survival business that I run:

Prepare and empower every American to protect their family, defend their freedom, and trust in God.

Our values:

> Treat every customer as if they were our own family member.
> Always do the right thing, regardless of what others say or think.
> Exercise honesty and integrity in all of our dealings.
> Keep the Sabbath day holy and don't work on Sunday.
> Never use foul or demeaning language.
> We are resourceful, we never give up, and we get it done no matter what it takes.
> Work hard and strive for greatness.
> Never stop learning about how we can keep people safer.
> We are grateful for our freedoms, which is why we strongly support the Second Amendment.

Intelligence officers take risks to protect us every single day; they uphold their vow to protect America, and they take this vow seriously. I feel it's just as important that I respect my own values and core beliefs when it comes to my business ventures.

My dedication to our core values was tested not long ago. A customer signed up for one of our advanced courses, which carries a heftier price tag than some of the others. He had decided to take the class after he had spent quite a bit of money buying various survival items from our website. Naturally, we were pleased when he signed up for the class, but then things got complicated. He started making excessive demands, yelling at my team and becoming irate if his emails weren't answered within minutes. In short, he turned out to be a difficult and unpleasant individual. Without an ounce of hesitation, I emailed him and thanked him for his business, but I calmly explained that, due to his behavior, he was no longer welcome in the class. I also refunded his fee of several thousand dollars. He was very surprised. But as I looked up past the computer and saw my values hanging on the wall, I knew I had done the right thing for my company and my team.

[SPY TIP]

OWN UP TO YOUR MISTAKES

When something goes wrong with an operation, the intelligence officer in charge takes full responsibility, no matter what happened and no matter whose fault it technically was. If a client is upset because my team messed up an order or made a mistake, in the end it's on me. I will own up to it and do everything in my power to appease that customer and make things right.

While I am honored to share what I've learned about business from my intelligence training, I can't tell you what feels wrong and right to you. That's personal and your choice. But I will say that having a zero-tolerance policy when it comes to difficult customers has enabled me to keep high-quality team members on board; it has virtually eliminated negativity from the work environment and has opened up time for us to seek out more fruitful opportunities. Whatever your belief system and wherever you are in the process of building your company, I highly recommend taking the time to lay out a mission statement and your core values. It doesn't have to be a million pages long, and it may evolve as your company grows, but it's immensely helpful to have principles to fall back on. When I was creating the mission statement and core values for Spy Escape & Evasion, I put time aside to ponder the following questions:

› How can we best serve people like nobody else in the industry?
› What is our ultimate goal?
› How will we achieve it?
› What is the value we will bring to our customers?
› What do we consider to be unacceptable?

Since the day I wrote down answers to those questions, I haven't had to second-guess myself. I never wonder if turning away a rude customer is the right thing; I know that keeping him on board is not something that's acceptable to me. Taking the time to execute this simple exercise has probably saved me countless hours dealing with pain-in-the-butt people and rightfully angry employees.

HOW TO TERMINATE THE RIGHT (AND SAFE) WAY

Being a former police officer and intelligence officer has taught me a few important lessons about dealing with difficult or irrational people. Most customers and clients who exhibit unacceptable behavior are most likely harmless, but I take the approach that each case should be handled carefully and calmly. I follow these steps once it's been determined that we must terminate a relationship with a customer:

Step One: Designate

Designate a person to execute the termination. At Spy Escape & Evasion, I am the only person who can terminate a customer. Depending on the size and scope of your company, figure out who has the authority, expertise and demeanor to do this professionally and carefully.

Step Two: Be Calm and Quick

Always remain calm, even if the customer is yelling and screaming. I know from experience that this can be difficult to execute, but you don't want to ignite their anger further. You don't need to spend an hour on the phone detailing everything they've done that has caused you to need to end the relationship. Also, always refund their money.

Step Three: Be Professional and Clear

Don't bother talking about how the person has made people at your company feel, or how this is their own fault. An unreasonable person will simply not see the part they played in this situation. Clearly state that they're no longer welcome to do business with your company.

Step Four: Stay Strong

Sometimes people apologize and swear they will change and that they really want to keep working together. Stick to your guns. This individual has already taken up lots of your valuable time and energy.

Step Five: Disengage

If the person sends an apology or an attack or tries to get in touch with your company in any way, do not engage with them. This is for your own safety and the safety of your employees. If someone is attempting to cause trouble or is angry, interacting with them will only push them. Much like you should avoid a stalker, you should never engage with an irrational client.

DON'T LET 20 PERCENT OF THE CLIENTS GIVE YOU 80 PERCENT OF THE GRIEF

While I'm grateful every single day that I took the plunge and started my own business, I will also tell you it's one of the hardest things I've ever done in my life. Running your own company is relentless, and, whether you expect it or not, there is always something to do. I believe this is why it's so incredibly important to spend some time thinking about your core values—and making a vow to follow them. I never forgot the oath I took as an intelligence officer on behalf of the United States of America. And as an entrepreneur and employer, I owe it to myself and my team members to follow through with those words hanging on my wall. To put it simply, I'm not going to let a handful of bad apples spoil the good thing we have going on at Spy Escape & Evasion. The next time you get an email or phone call from that dreaded client who is always stirring up trouble, consider whether or not it's truly worth engaging with them. Being an entrepreneur is hard enough; don't be afraid to send problem clients on their way so you can get back to doing the good work you really want to do.

[SPY MYTHS DECODED]

BEING A SPY IS ALL ABOUT NONSTOP ACTION. EACH DAY COULD INCLUDE ANYTHING FROM A HIGH-SPEED CAR CHASE TO A GUNFIGHT.

False!

If you look back at the story about Ryan and Thad, the most exciting moments were when Thad received a book or a hard-to-find part for his watch. Not terribly dramatic and probably very disappointing if you were expecting a shootout or a car chase. Since Ryan was doing his job right, it meant there was no drama—no guns drawn, no jumping off buildings or speeding away in a boat.

If Hollywood made a movie about what being a spy is usually like on a day-to-day basis, no one would want to see it. Being a spy involves incredibly detailed research, and this can take a long time. It also involves a lot of "casing," or following an individual to learn their habits and patterns of behavior. The planning stages of an operation could take months or even years—and that's a lot of time sitting at a desk. The truth is, if a spy finds himself in a fight, pulling out a weapon, or in a high-speed chase, it really means he's screwed up and gotten himself into a terrible situation. Good spying means not drawing attention to yourself.

PUTTING IT ALL TOGETHER

How I Used the SADR Cycle to Create Million-Dollar Marketing Campaigns

SPY TECHNIQUES IN ACTION

Since starting my own company, I've made millions of dollars selling survival and safety gear, books, and online courses, as well as by doing coaching sessions, speaking engagements, and, oddly enough, a Las Vegas stage show (in a million years I never could have seen that one coming). I'm not sharing this in order to brag, but because I want you to know that absolutely anyone can have the success I've had. By now, you should have a good understanding of how the various steps of the SADR cycle provide the perfect blueprint for finding the ideal customer, discovering what they *really* want, and convincing them that you're the person from whom to buy it.

When I started Spy Escape & Evasion, I didn't have any

fancy investors or employees to help me out, nor did I have business school experience to land me at a lofty starting place. What I *was* doing was working out of my apartment 24/7 to get things started. I had a fantastic service to offer, but I didn't have a single customer. Where would I find them? And once I did, how long would it take for me to transform them into a solid, repeat customer base? I knew my business could be a success if I could only connect with like-minded people who would appreciate my expertise.

Growing up, I had always loved the outdoors. I enjoyed hiking and camping, and I am even an Eagle Scout. I'm also an avid shooter and gun lover. I was well versed in survival tactics, and I believed that people would view me as a trusted resource. Since the only startup money I had was my own, I didn't want to spend a fortune on a newspaper ad or a commercial. Instead, I decided to view my new business as an important operation (and, let's face it, if it's your livelihood, it's an important operation). I'd look for customers the same way I would if I was looking for an asset who could share valuable information with the United States. In other words, I'd start with spotting.

ALLOW YOUR INTERESTS AND PASSIONS TO LEAD YOU TO YOUR CUSTOMER BASE

It was logical to let my hobbies and interests direct me to a place where I'd probably find like-minded people. I loved learning more about survival techniques, security, and guns, and chances were my customers did too. I made a list of all the gun shows, outdoor shows, and survival shows taking place throughout the United States. I wrote them all out on my calendar and made a point to go to every single one—**spotting** who was there and what they were doing. One day, I was walking through a survival show, weaving in and out of huge crowds of people, all of us looking at the latest and best developments in survival gear, when I realized what a fantastic opportunity this was. Nearly every person in this massive conference hall could potentially be my next best customer. But how did I transform these people from fellow survival enthusiasts to paying customers? I needed to discover what these people really wanted. What could I do that would get everyone to start buying from me? What element was missing that I could fill? What could I do better? I'd have to investigate further. Obviously, scouting for customers doesn't require the same stealth-like qualities of James Bond or the deductive skills of Sherlock Holmes, but I really wanted to maximize this opportunity. I'd have to use my intelligence training to **assess** the situation. I took note of the following:

The demographic: It was immediately obvious that most of the attendees were males about the ages of sixty and up. Only about 30 percent were women. There was no need to be scientific about this; I just needed a basic sense of who was attending these shows. Once you locate a place where your customers are likely to be, get a general sense of the demographics.

The purpose: I talked to as many people as I could about what brought them to the show. Most people whom I talked to came to the show because they strongly believed in self-reliance. They greatly valued freedom and supported the Second Amendment. The men wanted to have the best skills and resources when it came to protecting their families. Many of the women I talked to lived alone and wanted to ensure their own safety.

The big question: To make the most out of these opportunities, I asked people, "What is the number-one thing I could help you with right now?" Asking this open-ended question of a variety of people gave me a lot of information with which to work. Want to know the three biggest concerns people had? (1) How to protect their family from a home invasion. (2) Self-defense moves if some young punk tried to attack them in a parking lot. (3) Survival gear they should have at home and in their cars. People were basically opening up to me about their biggest fears and their greatest desires. I was able to gather so much information by asking this question that I ended up using it to collect more information when I started up my million-dollar internet marketing funnel (more on that later).

Case the scene: I paid attention to what other companies were present. I wanted to check out my competition. What kinds of services were other companies offering? What kinds of products were they pushing? Were there samples? How were they marketing their product? How were my offerings different or unique? What about my company could stand out? What kinds of people were drawn to which companies?

HOW TO USE THE INFORMATION YOU'VE COLLECTED TO SELL MILLIONS OF DOLLARS' WORTH OF MERCHANDISE AND/OR SERVICES: A STEP-BY-STEP GUIDE

Armed with information about who my ideal customer was, I started to **develop** my relationship with people who had concerns about safety and survival. I wanted to be the first person who popped into their heads when they thought about anything from water filtration in an emergency to evasive driving techniques. I wanted to be the go-to safety and survival guy. As you now know, developing is an art form that takes finesse and patience. I wasn't going to wreck my chances by bombarding people with information about everything I know. That would have been annoying (no one likes a know-it-all or spam email), difficult for me to execute, and, last, pointless. Developing a relationship, even a business relationship, is about personal connection. I wanted each person I contacted on my email list to feel like I was speaking directly to their worst fears or biggest wants. I wanted the parents of twin daughters who were concerned about safety and self-protection on college campuses to feel like I was personally addressing their concerns. I wanted women to feel like I understood their fears about protecting themselves when walking home alone at night. And while my goal has always been to provide helpful information that can potentially save a life, I also learned that it's possible to make a lot of money while doing exactly that.

Step One: Create a Website as a Selling Base for Your Product or Service

One fantastic thing about being an entrepreneur today is that it's not necessary to fork out thousands of dollars on a lease for a store or office space. You can make millions of dollars from a well-functioning website. Whatever it is you sell—tacos, dog-walking services, tutoring sessions, or handmade canoes, you need to create an irresistible offer. Whatever route you decide to take for building your website, once it's up and ready to go, the first thing you're going to do is give something away. Yes, that's right. You're going to give away a quality item for free. "Free" doesn't mean you're not going to make money. If you follow my advice, you're going to make more money than you ever imagined possible. (To get free website templates that I have used to generate seven-figure sales, visit www.SpymasterBook.com.)

Now, you're probably wondering where I got a list of people to contact by email. Well, the beautiful thing about the internet age is that when you know who your customers are, you can buy email lists of almost every group. For instance, I not only knew that my customers were aged sixty-plus and 70 percent male. I also knew they're conservative and watch Fox News and listen to people such as Glenn Beck and Rush Limbaugh. So I went and rented a bunch of conservative email lists, including many gun lists. (There are list brokers for pretty much every email list out there, so just find a list broker and tell them the type of customer you're looking to find.)

If you're wondering how to rent out your own email list without alienating your customers, I can tell you exactly how to do it. First, remember that the group "renting" your list doesn't get the actual names or email addresses. They receive one-time access to your list. They prepare the email they want your list to receive, and your company handles the actual distribution of the email. This is important for a couple of reasons: First, you're not sharing your customers' names or email addresses. That's a violation of trust. Second, I carefully vet the company who wants access to my list—and I test any product or service they're offering firsthand. I personally make sure that the product or service is something I would be willing to use myself. I stay clear of any get-rich-quick schemes or companies that don't come off in a professional manner. In the end, this process has brought products and services that I don't currently offer to my list of customers. It's the ultimate win-win.

QUICK AND EASY SPLIT TESTING

Split testing is also known as A/B testing, and it's just a way for marketers to try out two different versions of something to see which one makes a bigger impact. At Spy Escape & Evasion, we do split testing for everything: headlines, order forms, price points, pictures, et cetera. You don't have to conduct elaborate studies or use a huge sample for this technique to be useful. Create different headlines and take note of which one performs better, and then . . . *try to understand why*. Over time, you'll learn to perfect headlines and copy so that you're getting maximum results right away. I used to be one of the world's highest paid copywriters (when I wrote copy for many different companies) and have been fortunate to write for Agora publishing, among others.

Step Two: Select Something to Give Away for Free

Who doesn't love getting stuff for free? Giveaways send a signal that your company is generous and that you have so much faith in your product that you want to share it with the world.

I've given away copies of my books, video training, flashlights, tactical pens, and survival bags. All of these items are high quality and are a good example of the products and services my company offers. All I charge is a small shipping fee to cover the costs of delivery, since the Post Office doesn't give me free postage. For a hardcover book that normally sells for $27.95, a $5.95 shipping fee is almost nothing for the customer. This may sound counterintuitive, but giving something away has brought Spy Escape & Evasion so much additional income that we've made the giveaway part of our regular sales practice. We've found that giving away a free item does the following:

> **People talk:** Our spy flashlight is very compact. It's a mini light that you attach directly to a battery. It's so small it can fit in a woman's purse and take up no more room than a tube of lipstick. But it's powerful enough to be a lifesaver should you ever end up in the dark. Every time I pull mine out of my pocket (it fits easily), someone always says, "That's so cool, where did you get it?" And they're excited when I respond that it's free. Giving away our spy flashlights has resulted in many people hearing about our company for the first time. It creates buzz and word of mouth—great forms of advertising for your company.

> **Free items draw people in:** A free giveaway can be the final push that gets someone to buy something from you. If someone has been considering ordering a bug-out bag and all the gear but have been putting it off for whatever reason, that little free item can be the carrot that finally encourages them to drop by our site and take a look. A free item is an incredibly easy way to incentivize customers to visit your site.

Your company is associated with positivity: Customers who have been buying from us for a while have likely received many free, quality items from us. When they think of our company versus other companies who carry similar items, they remember these personal touches we give in the form of little gifts. Just like in the SADR cycle, this promotes a feeling of reciprocity, and people are more likely to continue buying from us.

You're getting people to test-drive your products: Even if someone had no intention of buying anything from us at all, they're still using one of our products. They'll have the opportunity to see firsthand that we seek out and sell the best, most useful survival products. Once they've seen what kinds of quality items we sell, it's likely they'll think of us in the future when the need to purchase something arises.

Step Three:
Recruit Customers by Creating an Irresistible Offer

At Spy Escape & Evasion, we do lots of giveaways. I'm certainly not the only company that offers something free as an incentive. Many companies do it because they know it works. There are countless products and services you can try for free, from Sirius satellite radio and video-streaming services to meal preparation kits and wardrobe subscriptions.

When we do giveaways, we list the offer on the front page of our site, in huge letters. This may sound obvious, but I'm always surprised by how many companies make people dig around for free offers. If a customer can't find it, it's pointless. We also have a quick but interesting video that automatically plays when someone visits the site. If the customer somehow didn't know we were giving away a free book or flashlight, trust me, they do now. Technology today makes it very easy to create a short but impactful video. I'm always sure to remember from my intelligence training that people absorb information in different ways. The text will draw some people, but others will be more likely to respond to the video.

Feature a Meaningful Testimonial

Get testimonials from regular people that describe the quality of your work.

When I was starting out, I got testimonials from people I felt others interested in the survival niche would admire—like Navy SEALs and army snipers.

> *"As someone who's worked operations with the CIA, I can tell you that Jason and his team are the real deal."*
> —Cade Courtley, former Navy SEAL

> *"Jason Hanson is a powerful proponent and practitioner of personal defense tools and techniques, all designed to protect you and your family."*
> —Peter Earnest, director of the International Spy Museum, and former CIA clandestine service officer

> *"It's a rare chance you get to learn from the best CIA operatives on how to stay alive in the crazy world we live in."*
> —Alain Burrese, former Army sniper

> *"Jason Hanson has forgotten more tradecraft than most will ever know."*
> —Rorke Denver, former Navy SEAL

If you own a taco truck, ask local parents to write something meaningful, such as "These tacos are so good my kids ask for them for dinner all the time." Never underestimate the power of a customer testimonial. If your customers are touting your business, people will listen. Trust is something a company earns, as is reliability. Having a testimonial from someone is just like having a "warm introduction" in the spy world. Someone else is vouching for your amazing services, and that's often enough to push someone to go ahead and check out what you have to offer for him- or herself.

Include a Bonus Item

If you're panicking that I'm asking you to give away yet another free item, hear me out. At Spy Escape & Evasion, we create webinars that contain highly valuable information. Creating this kind of additional content is fun, easy and can really help you **recruit** repeat customers. Think about something you can offer that will be irresistible to your target audience. If you sell pet supplies, consider creating a webinar about dog training techniques. Get creative, think about something that your customer will find useful or helpful. Even if you don't sell a physical product, you can still offer something terrific that people will want. If you're a mechanic, provide a prewinter checklist for keeping your car running smoothly. If you're a hair stylist, offer a free braiding seminar. Offer a free consultation—anything that can pique interest in your company.

Step Four: Introduce the Upsell Items

On the page where you click BUY NOW to claim the free item you are offering, explain that while you're giving the item away for free (and be sure to list the regular retail value), all you ask is that the customer pay the shipping and handling.

The appropriate information is asked for regarding shipping addresses and a credit card number. Once someone fills in their credit card number, they are immediately directed to an upsell, also known as a one-time offer (OTO). An OTO is where you make them a great offer on your other products and services. You can package items together to make them more appealing. You might want to offer a discount on your ultimate dog grooming tool or exclusive training session. Again, you'd want to feature a testimonial about why your service or tool is the best.

On our free book funnel, our first upsell is for our Sharpshooter University. Sharpshooter University is the premier destination for in-person and online firearms training and is the only organization in the world that gives you free live gun courses ($1,200 value). Members of this program receive monthly training videos, live gun courses, special reports, weekly intelligence alerts and our monthly printed newsletter called Spy & Survival Briefing. I have over 37,000 paid subscribers to my Spy & Survival Briefing newsletter (www .SharpshooterU.com) because I make it my mission to bring useful, valuable information that you can't find anywhere else. Several members have written to me to share that the information they learned by being part of the program has saved their lives.

Sharpshooter University leads customers to a second upsell. Our second upsell is for training videos that demonstrate how to execute all of the potentially lifesaving techniques from our live two-day Spy Escape & Evasion event. I explain that I hired a professional film crew to record the entire session and that this is the perfect solution for people who cannot attend the live event. (The live event is $1,500, so the videos are a more affordable option.) The third upsell is for the tactical pen, an easy-to-use, easy-to-carry self-defense tool that can save your life. Our final upsell is our home defense training program called Impenetrable Home Defense.

If You're Offering Upsells, You Must Be the Best in Your Industry

I can guess what you might be thinking, because chances are I've heard it before: Why so many upsells? Won't that turn a customer off? I've encountered other businesspeople who do online marketing and they've told me they don't feel comfortable offering so many upsells. I tell them the same thing every time: If you provide a quality product or service that tremendously helps people, you should be shouting about it from the rooftops. You should believe deep down that your product is so important that you need to get it into the hands of as many people as possible. I firmly believe that me and my team of ex-CIA officers are the best in the business when it comes to security, safety, and survival matters. We also have the track record to prove it. I know that when someone hires us for a security job or buys one of our products, they will undoubtedly be safer—the product could even save their life. Therefore, I never feel it is inappropriate to offer multiple upsells. If you ever feel badly about selling a service or an item, then you probably shouldn't be selling it at all.

[SPY TIP]

DON'T TRY TO BE EVERYTHING TO EVERYONE

I realize I've just told you to develop relationships, so you can tailor appropriate responses to different people. This is crucial, and I stand by my advice; however, understand that you can't be everything to everyone. There are always people who aren't going to want what you're selling. Don't waste valuable time and energy trying to convert people into buying an item or service that they just aren't on board with (even if you know deep down it might be the best thing for them). Too much time spent trying to broaden your customer base could end up costing you big in the end. If you have a niche business, don't be afraid to stick with it. Fellow *Shark Tank* alums have had great success with highly focused business ideas. As crazy as it sounds, Bombas socks, Scrub Daddy sponges, and even the Squatty Potty have been huge hits.

RECRUITING LIFELONG CUSTOMERS:
Be a Continued and Valued Presence

I'm proud to say that my survival company has thousands of repeat customers. Like I mentioned earlier, my Spy & Survival Briefing newsletter has over 37,000 paid subscribers. People who have received a free book or tactical pen end up buying spy flashlights or bug-out bags. People who take our introductory spy course often come back for our Ultimate Spy Week (www

.SpyWeek.com) or send their kids before they go off to college. Customers who have found some of our items valuable and helpful, like our survival water filter, end up buying them for their loved ones. Clearly, a repeat customer is the most valuable type of customer for any business. Regular customers become repeat customers when you continue to develop the relationship. Obviously, you're not necessarily going to be working the relationship by buying outlandishly expensive dinners like my CIA colleagues in the field sometimes do—but there are other easier, less costly, and authentic ways to continue working on a customer relationship.

STAY IN CONTACT WITH YOUR ASSETS

Other entrepreneurs tell me all the time that they don't like to send frequent emails to their followers and customers. They worry that the constant contact will get annoying and they'll end up losing customers. I don't agree with that approach at all. I worry about what will happen if *I'm not* in constant contact with my customers who are my greatest assets. I want to ensure that when a safety or survival need presents itself, Spy Escape & Evasion immediately comes to mind as a trusted resource. A spy in the field keeps in constant contact with assets because they definitely do not want that asset sharing valuable information with someone else—that just can't happen. We work hard to strike the proper balance and make sure we're providing our customers with appropriate communications. You'll have to determine a frequency that works best for your company, but at Spy Escape & Evasion we adhere to the following schedule:

SPY ESCAPE & EVASION
CUSTOMER CONTENT SCHEDULE

Monday: High-quality article. These pieces are about 500 words on a topic we know to be of interest to our customers. They are designed to be quick, informative reads. We've covered everything from how to build a survival shelter in the desert to how to protect yourself from various online scams.

Tuesday: Top five list. We'll craft an email that contains links to some of the most relevant articles on topics that appeal to our customer base.

Wednesday: A high-quality article, also approximately 500 words.

Thursday: We feature an article from one of my team members, often a former CIA buddy, about a topic that is interesting to them.

Friday: Another high-quality article from a Special Forces operator.

Saturday: Features the weekly mailbag, where I answer questions that are sent in by customers.

*YOU DON'T HAVE TO BE A PROFESSIONAL WRITER
TO CREATE QUALITY CONTENT*

If you love your niche and understand it, you shouldn't have trouble coming up with article ideas to share with your audience. You need to be a voracious reader who scans the news to be aware of any developments in your area. If writing makes you nervous, just think about it as writing an email to a friend—and essentially, that's what you're doing: You're communicating with your family of customers. If you really think you need help creating content, find a freelancer with whom you can connect to execute your ideas.

CONTINUE BUILDING CREDIBILITY WITH YOUR ASSETS:
Or, How I Ended Up Drinking Out of a Toilet in the Men's Room at McDonald's

As I've said, one of my biggest goals for Spy Escape & Evasion is for us to be the go-to resource for information about survival and safety. This isn't achieved by selling a person one tactical pen that they're happy about and they keep in their pocket at all times. While that's great, I want to go deeper and build longer lasting relationships. In the intelligence world, a spy's relationship with an asset needs to be so secure that the asset will do anything for you. I want to **recruit** our customers into our family of like-minded, self-reliant individuals who want the best, most up-to-date information about survival and safety.

I want our customers to know that I stand behind all of our products—that they work, they are reliable, and that I won't sell anything I don't use myself or I wouldn't let my family use. I practice what I preach, which is how I ended up doing a few things that most people would think were totally nuts. One of the biggest issues in an emergency is drinking water. Obviously, this is something a human being can't go without for very long—three days at the most. I always encourage people to keep a supply of water on hand: one gallon per person per day in your household, with a minimum supply of seven days but ideally enough to last for thirty days. But, being the good intelligence officer that I am, I always have a backup plan. My company sought out and now sells one of the best water-filtration systems available. I fully believe in this product—but I didn't want my word to stand alone. I wanted to build credibility by using it, and I did. I made a video of myself using the filter to drink out of the most disgusting water sources you can imagine. I wanted to prove that this device worked and was safe, and how better to prove it than by using the filter to drink the water directly out of a moss-covered and mosquito-infested pond, a trough at a farm (yes, it was used by the animals), and the toilet in the men's room at a McDonald's (and no, the last person to use it had not flushed). The filter worked, the water tasted clean, and I did not get sick. I didn't make this video to shock people. I made it to show my valued customers (**assets**) that I'm not going to mess around with their well-being and safety by selling an inferior product.

CONNECT WITH STORIES

I love my company's tactical pen. It's a solid weapon that can save your life, but it's also a pen and I use it all the time for regular things like signing papers. Because it's essentially a pen, that also means you can take it anywhere. I always tell people that the safest way to fly (other than following all the travel safety tips I've written about in *Spy Secrets That Can Save Your Life*), is to carry on a tactical pen. Obviously, you can't take a real weapon on a plane, but you can take a pen. This could be used for self-defense purposes should someone try something crazy. It's also a great weapon to have on you when you're traveling in an unfamiliar city. But people are nervous to do this—they're afraid the pen won't get through security. Or, worse, they'll get in trouble for trying to take a weapon on a plane. But when a client reached out to me to tell me how pleased he was to have his tactical pen with him on a recent trip to Israel, I was very curious. El Al Airlines is known for its incredibly tight security. Yet he had no problem taking the pen on board. I immediately shared this story with my customers. Here it is:

> I travel quite a bit (within the states and internationally) and the idea of having at least some form of weapon available at all times is comforting. I just went through the safest airport in the world (Ben Gurion in Israel) and I carried my pen with me at all times. Never once an issue, no questions when it was x-rayed, and some peace of mind for me. Traveling alone to new (and strange) countries can be a little scary. But at least I don't feel unarmed now.

I wanted them to see firsthand how it is possible to empower yourself with this pen while traveling, and this story showed that it was completely possible. To continue being seen as the go-to person for whatever your product is, you sometimes need to share stories about other people's experiences. Stories are how we connect as human beings, and sharing them can have a great impact on how your customers connect with you.

SHARE YOUR OWN EXPERIENCES

I like to share stories about my own personal experiences with survival and safety. While I'm not interested in making material all about me, I do think it's important to talk about instances where I've been put in positions to use my own techniques or tools. I want to let my readers and customers see me using my expertise out in the real world. I've talked about how my experience running with the bulls in Pamplona gave me a good look at what a complete meltdown of society might feel like. When you're running in a crowd being chased by a thousand-pound animal with horns, all social politeness goes out the window. I've written about the advice I gave to a family member who had the horrible experience of being stalked. I've talked at length about how I've taught my toddler daughter about gun safety; I shared a letter I wrote to her that I want her to read when she's older and buys her first gun. Then there was the time my wife and I heard a terrible sound in the middle of the night—and I found myself casing the house with my gun out, only to discover the culprit was a suitcase that had fallen from a shelf. I'm not the most public person, but if something is going on in my life that could be relevant to my audience from a safety and survival perspective, I share it.

Always ask them what they want: Once again, I go back to the big question. I provide a small questionnaire on the company website. And I recommend always ending the questionnaire by asking about the number-one thing that can help a customer right now. The information you get from this simple question will prove invaluable. You can also take the answers and customize content that appeals to different groups of people with specific interests.

Here's an example of what I ask. It is easy to tailor this survey to any type of business.

> What is the number-one thing I can do for you to help you and your family stay safer this year?
> Which topics do you wish to learn more about?
>   - Home protection
>   - Guns
>   - Food storage
>   - Self-defense
>   - Cyber security
>   - Natural disaster preparation
>   - Other
> Where do you usually go for information about these topics?
> What can I help you with right now?

ESSENTIAL COMPONENTS OF THE MILLION-DOLLAR SALES FUNNEL

Multiple upsells: Quite simply, different people respond and buy different upsells. Including a mix of items increases your chances of making money.

Good sales copy: We've worked hard at Spy Escape & Evasion to develop wording that sparks an interest in our customers. It's crucial to have well-written copy that creates a sense of value and urgency. Don't create a great-looking website and not use polished, professional copy. As I mentioned, I used to be one of the world's highest paid copywriters and wrote for Agora, among others. These days, I only write copy for myself and my coaching clients (www.Spymasterbook.com). However, the ability to write copy is one of the most important skills you can have. It's just like using the SADR cycle, but you're doing it on paper instead of in person.

Quality content: Always aim to provide that extra bit of information that others aren't giving. Consistently providing valuable content leads to your becoming the number-one trusted resource for whatever product or service you sell.

At Spy Escape & Evasion, we've used the elements of the SADR cycle to create dozens of successful marketing campaigns that have brought in millions of dollars. Running your own business is one of the most rewarding and also the most difficult endeavors a person can take on. Following the SADR cycle process can lighten the load by introducing your business to lucrative new revenue streams. I realize at first that this might seem complicated and time consuming. Trust me that it gets easier as you refine your technique—and the positive results make all the effort well worth it. If, like me, you're incredibly proud of the products and services you offer, then you should maximize their potential by creating this simple and successful system. I hope you'll soon see, like I have, that the possibilities here are endless.

[SPY MYTHS DECODED]

SPIES ARE HIRED FROM ALL WALKS OF LIFE AND DIFFERENT EDUCATIONAL BACKGROUNDS.

True!

One of the most fascinating things about being an entrepreneur is meeting other businesspeople with so many different backgrounds. I've met successful businesspeople who started out as comedians, lawyers, or even circus performers. The intelligence world is similar—people come from a variety of fascinating and different backgrounds. Just like many successful entrepreneurs don't have an MBA, and contrary to what people might think, Ivy League schools are not a breeding ground for future spies. While intelligence officers are certainly some of the smartest folks I know, the CIA values and respects individuals from a variety of backgrounds. The famous Tony Mendez depicted in the movie *Argo* studied art in college. He answered an ad for a job as a graphic designer and ended up getting hired by the CIA. The famous chef and cookbook writer Julia Child worked as a copywriter at an ad agency in New York City before she joined the OSS (Office of Strategic Services, the predecessor to the CIA) as a typist. She eventually was entrusted with top-secret research. Many intelligence officers have chosen to join the military rather than go to college (I got my start as a police officer). And if you were to sit down with a group of spies and ask them what the strangest job they've ever had is, I assure you that you'd get some interesting answers, including florist, taxi driver, and even cowboy. The CIA is more interested in a person's overall intelligence and ability to quickly solve problems than they are an Ivy League degree. Overall intelligence and ability is starting to matter more in business too. According to a recent CNBC study, the majority of small business owners do not have a four-year college degree. Businesspeople who didn't attend college outnumbered those who did across both genders and all age groups. It's great to have access to education, but running a successful business is about much more than a piece of paper.

PART TWO

Spy Skills Equal Common Sense on Steroids:
How Enhanced Common Sense Will Take Your Business to New Heights

One of my most brilliant colleagues who dutifully served our country as an intelligence officer for years puts it best: "Spy skills are just common sense on steroids." Boiled down to its simplest form, he's absolutely right. Intelligence training is about learning to home in on innate skills—refining, developing, and perfecting them until they reach a very heightened sense. It requires spending years of your life learning to elevate common sense to something bigger and more powerful. When you learn to do this, how you view the world and your immediate environment changes. You understand that at the foundation of any successful mission are some key concepts. No mission would succeed without loyalty, teachability, communication, and preparedness. It's common sense that we should go through life valuing our friends, family, and co-workers, and we should keep our minds open to new concepts, communicating appropriately in our daily interactions and preparing ourselves for unforeseen happenings. In the spy world, those common sense concepts mean absolutely everything—these simple ideas represent the difference between success and failure as well as life and death.

Since leaving the CIA and becoming an entrepreneur, I've seen how these same basic concepts are a perfect guide to running a business. If you can learn to tap into your common sense and allow it to grow to unprecedented levels, it will be your own personal compass, steering your company toward greatness.

CHAPTER 8

NEXT-LEVEL LOYALTY

In the CIA, the relationship between partners is unique. An operation can send you and your partner into the depths of the most hostile countries where Americans simply aren't welcome. You're charged with completing a dangerous mission, and you have only each other to depend on. While sometimes intelligence officers work in teams on certain operations, more often than not it's a very small group and you are also often alone. We're not the military—there's no cavalry. And now you know that if you're in covert operations, the government isn't going to come in and retrieve you should something (or everything) go wrong. This results in a loyalty so deep and meaningful it can be hard for people who haven't been in the intelligence world to understand it.

ELLIOT'S STORY

I will never forget the time I thought I had let my partner down (literally, over the side of a roof). We needed to get on top of a building in a hostile territory to plant a listening device. Of course, we didn't want to get spotted, so we chose a night during which we knew the moon would be out. The moonlight would be our only light as we executed the necessary maneuvers. Well, it turns out there was zero moonlight. We couldn't see our hands in front of our faces up there. My partner, Mark, tripped over a wire. I didn't see this, so I had no idea what had happened at the time, but it made a loud noise. We had worked together long enough to know that darkness combined with a sudden noise was a good reason to abort the mission. We had to get out rather than risk being caught. I didn't know where Mark was, but I knew I had to get back to the escape vehicle. I had to assume that's where I'd find him too. I got down from the roof and realized he was nowhere to be found. I started to panic because I had removed the ladder. Did Mark get caught? It was my duty to find him and help him if he needed it. I quietly climbed back up to the roof. As I surveyed the perimeter, I thought I saw a dark shadow. It was either Mark or someone who had figured out what we were doing and who was coming for my life. Luckily, it was Mark. He had fallen and was literally hanging over the side of the building. I was so grateful I had made it in time to pull him up before his arms gave out. Horrible things would have been done to me if I had gotten caught (and remember, I had made it to the escape vehicle), but there was no way I'd leave my partner behind. Doing so was unthinkable.

NEXT-LEVEL LOYALTY BREEDS SUCCESS

Loyalty in the intelligence world has a very specific meaning. When you are put in a partnership situation in the intelligence world, you're opening yourself up to the idea that your life and well-being may fall into another person's hands. You realize that, should certain circumstances arise, whether or not you wake up the next day is up to your partner. This requires knowing you would do the same—that you'd do anything to keep your partner safe. Out in the field, your partner is your family. And you'll do anything for your family. This is the highest level of loyalty I have ever experienced. Now that I'm an entrepreneur, I don't imagine I'll ever have to rescue one of my employees who is hanging from a building (or vice versa), but what I learned about loyalty in my intelligence training has made a huge impact on how I conduct my life and run my business.

WHAT DOES LOYALTY MEAN TO YOU IN THE WORKPLACE?

When I was ready to grow my business and start working with team members, I needed to reassess what loyalty meant to me in the workplace. While my life wouldn't depend on the actions of my employees, my livelihood would. The reverse was also true. My employees were counting on me to run a thriving, successful business so that they could depend on their income. They were trusting me to provide them with a productive, safe, and even fun workplace environment. I realized that in the business world, next-level loyalty required me to think of my team members as family. I had already established what my core principles would be, but how would I hold myself accountable to those principles? I vowed that in order to uphold the culture I wanted to create—one that bred next-level loyalty—I would have to commit to the following:

> **Commitment to the mission:** I'd have to consistently demonstrate that I was committed to our company's mission. I'd have to openly show my willingness to do whatever it took to steer the ship forward and build a company for myself and my team members. In the intelligence world, both partners must be fully committed to completing an operation. They'll do anything and work relentlessly to make it happen. I'm always the first at work and the last to leave, consistently demonstrating my dedication to the success of the business.

> **Transparency:** I'd have to be transparent about the state of the business whenever possible. Team members would need to be briefed on new opportunities, changes in the company, successes, failures, what's going on with our competition, and our goals. Partners out in the field openly share all of their intelligence about a mission, as this is the only way to get the job done. Partners don't

withhold information from each other, as secrets can put
the entire operation at risk.

**Recognizing and accepting the strengths and weaknesses of
each individual:** Every intelligence officer brings something
unique to the table. The CIA functions due to the myriad
of skills and talents into which the agency can tap. The
agency hires some of the country's best and brightest,
but you might be surprised by how wildly our talents
vary. There are experts on toxins and poisons, masterful
forgers, snipers, linguists, psychologists, accountants,
coders, artists. Without people who excel in all of these
different backgrounds, we wouldn't be able to collect the
intelligence and execute the missions to keep America safe.
Each member is valued for their distinct contribution.
I realized I would make a point to honor and respect
each person's strengths—and accept that weaknesses are
human and not necessarily flaws that need to be fixed.
I have team members who are fantastic writers, others
who are incredibly organized planners, patient and kind
customer service people, and top-notch security people. By
respecting and recognizing everyone's contribution to Spy
Escape & Evasion, I'm allowing people to put their best
foot forward, which makes us stronger as a team.

Standing up for my team: One of the reasons I'm willing to
terminate relationships with overly difficult customers
is out of loyalty to my hardworking team members. If I
want to encourage next-level loyalty, I need to prove that
their well-being and state of mind mean more than a
quick profit. During my time in the CIA I would never

have hesitated to stand up for my partner in a crisis. I wanted my team members to know that, without a doubt, they would be appropriately supported and cared for in difficult situations.

Rewarding excellent behavior: Spies understand that their assets are putting themselves at risk in bringing them useful information. Spies show gratitude for their assets whenever they can by providing big-ticket items or smaller rewards such as dinners and cash. Likewise, I am always going to recognize when someone has gone above and beyond. I will never forget how my team came together last Christmas when our orders were through the roof and getting those shipments out was a huge challenge. Without my insisting in any way, the team gathered on Saturdays and late at night, helping to prepare and package orders for shipping. Without their willingness to pitch in, we could have lost out on a lot of business. I was happy to reward my team in the form of meals, gifts, and bonuses. If you want next-level loyalty, always make a point of acknowledging extraordinary behavior, even if it's something as simple as helping to pack up last-minute Christmas orders.

Doing unto others as you would have them do unto you: This is the simplest of all statements but perhaps the most powerful. I wanted to be the kind of leader who earned the respect of his team members by being ethical, pursuing excellence, being respectful, and always showing integrity. I wanted to model good behavior as well as treat everyone on my team as I want to be treated myself. Intelligence officers cannot work together if they do not mutually respect each other. There's no room for arguing or mistrust out in the field, and a mission won't be completed without a joint commitment to excellence and integrity.

When you're completing your training with a group of other intelligence officers, integrity is essential. Your partner is in charge of saving your life. During training I'd think, Who in this group would I trust with my life? Anyone who wasn't a good shot, was a hothead, or didn't collaborate well was a liability. Those people often did not make it through training because they put the rest of the group in danger. I view my company in a similar fashion: Every member has a key role to play. Their contribution is essential to the livelihood of the company. Obviously, human beings make mistakes, and I don't expect perfection, but *integrity matters*. I had one employee who was smart, likable, and did great work. The only problem? He couldn't meet deadlines. This individual wasn't respecting the rest of our team by doing his work in a timely fashion. He was becoming a liability. I talked to him about this problem and said I'd do whatever I could to help because he did such good work. In the end, he couldn't deliver on time and, for the sake of the team, I had to let him go. Show your commitment to integrity by honoring the core values you've established. Not insisting on integrity from every team member is dangerous to the survival of your company.

LOYALTY STARTS WITH YOU

I had been taught that when you're devoted to a cause (such as the success of a new business or protecting the United States of America), you develop a deep appreciation for every part of the process. In the CIA we value the analysts, the cartographers, the mechanics who work on our cars, the administrative staff, and even the employees in the coffee shop who make the hot chocolate on those cold northern Virginia days. You see how crucial each component is to running a successful organization. That deep appreciation for each part of the process, and the pride you feel about providing your own personal contribution, is where loyalty begins to grow. As I began to build Spy Escape & Evasion, I was able to immediately appreciate each team member's contribution to the whole.

CHAPTER 9

EXTREME PREPARATION

Prepare and Prepare Again

Benjamin Franklin, a founding father of this country who also managed to invent bifocals and the lightning rod, publish the first political cartoon, and become one of the five men to draft the Declaration of Independence, said it best: "By failing to prepare, you are preparing to fail." Throughout my various careers, I've placed a lot of value on preparation; I've practically elevated it to an art form.

At the agency we had bug-out bags. These bags were equipped with everything you would reasonably need to survive should a major attack occur. We were taught to check, check, and recheck our bug-out bags on a regular basis. Should a catastrophe take place, you didn't want to be the guy who didn't have extra batteries for his radio and couldn't communicate with anyone. We were taught to approach the planning of missions in the same way. After reading a requirement, we didn't just jump into action. We double-checked and dug deeper with the analyst who wrote the requirement, so we could ensure we understood everything and could make the right preparations. No intelligence officer wants to head out to a remote part of a foreign country only to find out he doesn't have everything he needs. In that case he can't exactly walk into a local store and buy a super powerful antenna capable of picking up enemy chatter. If the preparations aren't executed perfectly, the mission will fail.

Preparation saves lives. We've all seen horrible stories on TV about what the lack of preparation does when a natural disaster such as a hurricane hits—people die from lack of water. People die out in the elements when they get lost during a blizzard and don't have the right gear. I have always prepared myself and my family properly so that we can survive any attack or natural disaster. As any entrepreneur knows, starting a new business is terribly risky. According to the Bureau of Labor Statistics, 20 percent of new businesses fail in the first year, and 50 percent in the second year. Those are scary numbers. It was a great gift when I realized that my natural inclination toward preparation (*extreme preparation*, anyone who knows me would say) could be the factor that fail proofs my business.

THE POWER OF CHECKLISTS

At Spy Escape & Evasion, we have carefully crafted checklists for every class we teach, and they are extremely detailed. It's easy to underestimate how helpful a checklist can be when conducting business, but they are much more than a few words scribbled on a piece of paper. A strong checklist system can provide your business with some excellent benefits:

Training tools: New employees can refer to checklists and easily see what the expectations are for a specific task and can see all the steps required to successfully execute a task.

Maintain consistency: At Spy Escape & Evasion, we know exactly what is needed to make each of our events safe and enjoyable for our customers—our classes are consistent. The only people who teach our courses are experienced former intelligence officers who are the tops in their field. Our spy exercises are always executed in fun and lively locations—from the streets of a small town to Las Vegas casinos. We are always sure to include a memorable exercise. Duct taping people's hands together and teaching them how to escape from a locked trunk is always a hit. And we work hard to make sure our presentations are fresh and easy to understand. Our lectures are accompanied by dynamic visual presentations to make sure we're delivering our message in ways that everyone can understand.

Help delegate: We can refer to a checklist when we're planning an event and instantly see all of the tasks that need to be taken care of. This is incredibly useful when deciding which team members are going to tackle what tasks. We can also instantly see if an event requires more hands on deck and we can bring in extra help.

Open up time for other activities: Having everything laid out for you in a checklist allows you to perfect your technique and leaves you with more energy for other tasks. Knowing you have a flawless system for executing something relieves stress and opens up time for everything from networking to goal setting.

CHECKLISTS PROVIDE INVALUABLE FEEDBACK:
The After-Action Report

It's true that before an event I'll triple-check that every item on my list is accounted for (and I'll probably go ahead and check everything one more time). I'll carefully load the truck with gear the night before the event, crossing items off as they're packed. If we're doing a shooting class, I'll check the number of firearms, ammunition, targets, hearing protection, shooting glasses, QuikClot (in case of an emergency), radios, batteries, bullhorn, water, sandwiches, snacks, and so forth. One missing item can mean the difference between an amazing experience and a mediocre one. I'll also have called the hotel to check on the accommodations for people who are flying in. If we're using a conference room for meetings, I'll confirm the lighting, the electrical outlets, and the seating format. This is the easiest yet most important thing you can do to ensure success for your business. But there's an additional value to extreme preparation: It also provides you with easy, free, instant feedback about how to improve your experience for even greater success in the future. In the field, spies are going to be carefully tracking their progress. Depending on the nature of the operation, they may be taking notes, communicating via radio, or writing secrets down on water-soluble paper (which will dissolve easily if a spy needs to destroy it quickly). Spies are always refining their process—

paying attention to what has worked, techniques that need to be improved, and tactics that were smoothly executed and worked well. All of this information is carefully documented in what's known as the after-action report (AAR). An after-action report is a document used to review any project or event after its completion. It's useful for learning about what went right, noting what went wrong, and helping to ensure a better outcome next time.

For example, if you work in real estate, you're going to be holding lots of open houses for other realtors and the public. Your ability to sell a home (and ultimately earn a commission) is dependent on those open houses running smoothly. Imagine the impression you'd make if you couldn't open the door because you forgot the key. What if the brochures you had printed weren't ready in time? Or, worse, what if you opened the door minutes before the open house was due to begin and discovered the occupants had had some wild party and the house was a huge mess? Having a process—namely, checklists detailing everything required to make the event a success, from brochures to a process for making sure the house is in order—can make the difference between closing a sale (and getting new clients from people who are impressed by how you work) and having a disastrous event.

THE COMPANY BRIEFING:
How to Create an After-Action Report

We have a teamwide briefing after every event. We sit down to discuss the event in detail, and we go over every aspect of our after-action report. This is exactly what intelligence officers do after an operation. They are always analyzing and carefully refining procedures so that future operations will run even more smoothly. The after-action report is one of the most impactful tools we have to assess and evaluate our events. We are always on the lookout for ways to improve the customer experience, become more efficient, and fill in any gaps that could cause problems. A good AAR generally looks like the following:

[EXERCISE SUMMARY]

SPY ESCAPE & EVASION

EXERCISE NAME: Ultimate Spy Week

EXERCISE DATES: September 10, 2017–September 16, 2017

SUMMARY/SCOPE OF EXERCISE:

OBJECTIVES: They Ultimate Spy Week is an adrenaline-charged week that teaches attendees the following skills: escape & evasion, evasive driving, knife defense, riflecraft, pistolcraft, and hand-to-hand combat. Our goal is to have every attendee leave with the confidence and skills to overcome any threat they face.

POTENTIAL THREATS/HAZARDS: We have switched the venue to a new hotel—it's crucial we confirm the seating arrangement we've requested has been executed. Confirm audiovisual equipment is set up and working. Also, we're using a new area for practicing surveillance detection routes. Last, and perhaps most pressing, is that we ensure safety during the breaking out of a trunk exercise. We want to alert authorities in the area—do not want to be mistaken for actual kidnapping.

Participating individuals:
Eight team members from Spy Escape & Evasion

1. Jason Hanson
2. Instructor X
3. Instructor Y
4. Instructor Q

5. Instructor S
6. Audiovisual
7. Admin
8. Admin

CORE CAPABILITY №1:

A. Strengths—Instructor X was captivating and informative; his presentations were lively and well received.
   1. Visuals. Created clarity.
   2. Storytelling. Compelling and useful.
   3. Skills. Well executed and easy to follow.
B. Area for improvement:
   1. Cover stop explanation should come earlier in presentation.
   2. More props would improve the presentation further.

CORE CAPABILITY №2: HOTEL/NEW VENUE

A. Strengths
   1. Attendees greeted appropriately and given directions.
   2. Room set up as requested.
   3. Audio and visual working as requested.
B. Area for improvement:
   1. Lower floor would be better; took too long for people to go downstairs for food or drinks during breaks.
   2. Temperature of the room inconsistent.

CORE CAPABILITY №3: ADMIN

A. Strengths
   1. Checked in with all participants. Made everyone feel welcome.

2. Handled logistical problems with any guests.

3. Took photographs of participants doing training exercises.

B. **Area for improvement:**

1. Give out photo-release forms before arrival.

2. Offer to email photos to participants who want them.

3. Consider bringing second camera so two people can shoot.

4. The water went quickly. Two more cases of bottled water should be purchased for next event.

THE ANATOMY OF AN AFTER-ACTION REPORT

Whether we've just concluded one of our week-long spy courses or we've finished a major project such as designing, manufacturing, and selling a new knife, we'll recap our objectives in an AAR. While we've crafted our own after-action report that suits our needs, it's easy to create one that works for your business. To ensure you're getting as much valuable information as possible, consider including the following summary.

SUMMARY OF THE PROJECT/ RECAP OF OBJECTIVES

What was the ultimate goal?

Our goal was to design, manufacture, market, and sell a high-quality survival knife that could be used in covert operations. It had to be lightweight and use only the finest steel on the market. Also had to have a modular sheath, allowing the user to wear the knife multiple ways on his person.

Was that goal reached?
After consulting with several designers, we landed on a concept that met our criteria. We were also able to locate a strong, lightweight steel that fit in with our pricing parameters.

What parts of the project/event worked?
Designer X was easy to work with, affordable, communicated clearly, and followed through with everything he said he was going to do. He is a fantastic asset, and his contributions to the project helped us reach our goal.

What parts didn't work? Why?
It was more challenging to find the right steel, and get enough supplies to meet the high demand. We will have to monitor this consistently.

What elements need to be changed?
Initially, this project took more time than anticipated, as we needed to locate the right designers, producers, and vendors. We need to do more outreach to have quicker access to people working in these areas.

Briefing takeaway:

> List conclusions drawn after everyone has read the AAR.
> Discuss who will be responsible for which actions.
> Offer opportunity for team members to voice opinions or ideas.
> Make any appropriate changes to the checklist.

Checklists and AARs can help you avoid annoying, costly mistakes that can result in your losing a customer. Intelligence officers are not the only people who have faith in checklists. Surgeon and author Atul Gawande has written extensively about how checklists save lives. As a surgeon, he notes that there are "errors of ignorance" and "errors of ineptitude." The first error stems from making mistakes because we don't know something, the second because we aren't using what we know in the right way. He wisely points out that most failures are due to the second form of ignorance. Checklists and AARs are a simple solution that can prevent the constant mistakes that can arise simply because we are human. Surgeons and pilots heavily rely on such systems for this reason.

And perhaps the best part of this system? After I've carefully loaded a truck the night before an event—crossing off each item as I've packed it—I know I can go to bed and enjoy a stress-free night of sleep, because I know with 100 percent certainty that everything my team needs for a successful event is right where it needs to be.

SPY MYTHS DECODED

SPIES DON'T WEAR TRENCH COATS IN REAL LIFE, IT'S JUST IN THE MOVIES.

False!

It usually seems ridiculous to see a spy in a full-length trench coat. In the movies they're always running after someone or being chased, obviously being impeded somewhat by the coat they're wearing. But the truth is, the classic spy trench coat is the best garment for carrying around all of the tools necessary to do the job. As I've just told you, spies are perhaps the most prepared people in the world. Their trench coat is likely to have specially created compartments that hold a firearm, knives, ammunition, a flashlight, a phone, a radio, and canisters to contain information. Depending on the level of danger, it's possible that secret compartments would have been added into the coat so that the intelligence officer can safely transport top-secret information.

[AFTER ACTION REPORT TEMPLATE]

EXERCISE SUMMARY

EVENT/PROJECT:

DATES:

SUMMARY/SCOPE OF EVENT/PROJECT:

OBJECTIVES:

POTENTIAL COMPLICATIONS:

PARTICIPATING TEAM MEMBERS:

CORE CAPABILITY №1:

A. Strengths
    1.
    2.
    3.

B. Area for improvement:
    1.
    2.

CORE CAPABILITY №2:

A. Strengths
    1.
    2.
    3.

B. Area for improvement:
    1.
    2.

CORE CAPABILITY №3:

A. Strengths
    1.
    2.
    3.

B. Area for improvement:
    1.
    2.
    3.
    4.

CHAPTER 10

ALWAYS BE TEACHABLE

Conrad Hall, the renowned cinematographer who has shot such classic movies as *In Cold Blood, Cool Hand Luke,* and *Butch Cassidy and the Sundance Kid* (to name just a few), believed passionately in the power of learning. While he had mastered his craft and worked with some of the biggest movie stars and directors of his time, he always felt there was much more to learn. "You are always a student, never a master," he said. "You have to keep moving forward." This sentiment holds true in the intelligence world, and it has set me on a path to remain open and flexible as I've built my own business. I like to think of intelligence training as learning from a long line of masters. I've been incredibly fortunate to have learned my spy skills from gifted individuals who practice their craft with caution, pride, and a strong sense of excellence. These people, too, have been taught by gifted professionals—and on down the line it goes.

It is also true that everyone in this learning chain has a good-sized ego (a fairly big ego is required to carry out an intelligence operation or to run a business of any size). You need to exude confidence, be a leader, make quick decisions, and be ready to take full responsibility when something goes wrong. However, I am confident that myself and every teacher with whom I've had the honor of working will agree on one thing: You can never stop learning. In the espionage world, the moment you deem yourself "a master" you're putting yourself (and your team members) at great risk. In fact, one of my most esteemed colleagues who taught at the Farm says, "One of the best qualities a recruit can have is an ability to take criticism. This isn't all about you, it's about the mission—the outcome. When you're out in the field you're always gathering information. We do this because we know that information has the ability to save lives. The second you think you know everything, you're through." It's the same with business. An entrepreneur must lead with confidence, make the tough choices, decide which risks to take, and know that when something goes wrong, *it's on you.* If you reach a point where you do not accept the wisdom of others and you aren't open to learning new skills from those who possess different gifts, that's when you're placing a ceiling on how much your company can achieve. To encourage my team members (and myself, of course) to remain teachable, I suggest practicing the following:

> **Be a good listener:** Spies are excellent listeners. This is one of the best lessons a businessperson can take from espionage. By listening, you are learning, and you never know when you're going to hear that bit of information

ALWAYS BE TEACHABLE   193

about a company you're curious about, a product you want to sell, or a contact you want to meet. Prioritize listening over sharing.

Remain open to criticism: Each of us has our own unique gifts and talents. It's an honor to have the opportunity to learn from others who have different strengths, experiences, and backgrounds.

Be willing to change yourself: Many of us would prefer to change the rules or change the course of how a business operates rather than change ourselves. If you can't blend and make sacrifices as an intelligence officer, you'll be killed. In business, sometimes we have to take a moment and acknowledge we are the ones who need to change— not our sales team, our marketing department, or our employees. Things don't always operate in a manner that suits our own needs, and sometimes we simply have to adapt. Spies never settle for reusing the same approach when recruiting assets or developing an alias. Take a cue from the intelligence world and make a point of adding new skills, exploring new viewpoints, and being flexible.

THERE IS A FINE LINE BETWEEN RISK AND FAILURE: The Toxic Ego

It is always easy to accept that we all have limits, but intelligence officers are taught to push themselves to achieve more and do better while also respecting individual limits. Spies aren't superhuman, and anyone who makes the mistake of believing they are will likely fail. Tom Cruise's character Ethan

Hunt of the aptly named Impossible Missions Force does everything from free-climb cliffs to hang off the side of airplanes midair. While I've known spies who have saved their lives by diving into rivers in the dark of night to avoid a knife fight, I don't know any who would make the mistake of thinking they could hold their breath underwater for six minutes (which Ethan Hunt also does). In espionage as well as in business, the fine line between taking a risk and going too far and failing is determined by the size of one's ego. I've seen time and again how a big ego can destroy a deal. Walking away from an inappropriate or undoable offer is one thing, but walking away from something because of an unreasonable view of your singular value to the situation is a terrible mistake. To keep your mission moving in a constructive direction, you have to avoid developing a toxic ego (and avoid working with people who have one whenever possible). Make a point to carefully consider the following:

> **Analyze negative feedback:** We've all worked with customers who will never be happy. Technology makes it very easy for someone to leave a negative review of a product or service. It's an unfortunate part of running any business. But if you find yourself immediately dismissing all criticisms, you need to take pause. Feedback about products, employee performance, and customer service is always valuable, whether it's from a brand-new employee, a VP who has decades of experience, or a new customer.

> **You can't control everything:** Being a self-starter is a crucial quality in an intelligence officer. The CIA can't check in on its people every single day. Nothing would be achieved. The CIA trains its people well, knows certain personality traits

work well for espionage, and then lets the intelligence officers do their jobs. Accepting that your teammates are capable of doing their jobs and giving them the space and power to do so is crucial to their success.

You can't work only with people who agree with you: The CIA carefully pairs partners. Each needs to enhance the other's skills and abilities, as this is the best way to put intelligence officers in the position to complete successful operations (and stay alive). Imagine two partners in hostile territory readily agreeing on every move and every decision. It might sound great at first—but complete agreement means there's no discourse. It eliminates healthy discussions about things like why it's not a great idea to scale a foreign government's building in broad daylight or why it's not a good idea to overextend a business and buy two warehouses. If everyone is agreeing with you about everything, it's likely you've put yourself in a situation that is supportive of a toxic ego.

You set goals that are unattainable: Whenever intelligence officers receive a requirement from an analyst, it's their duty to execute it. Thousands of lives could be at stake. That's why it's crucial that in intelligence work everyone understands what's "attainable." Sure, we're taught to push and take risks—but not at the expense of destroying an entire operation. I admire lofty goals, and as an entrepreneur I set the bar high for myself; but as an intelligence officer, I know how arrogance and ego can pull a person to inflate goals. Flying too high, both in espionage and the business world, can have grave consequences.

I'm fortunate that the individuals who have trained me have gone above and beyond in sharing their valuable skill-set experiences and wisdom, but they've also given me something bigger. They've demonstrated how critical it is to remain teachable and to maintain a healthy ego at all times. I wouldn't have had success if I hadn't been open to listening and learning. I've trusted the experience and expertise of the people I've partnered with, who have shown me the ropes in those areas and helped me achieve new things. I've learned firsthand that if you aren't finding yourself in situations where you don't know everything and need someone else to guide you, then you're just not pushing yourself enough. Plunge yourself into unknown waters, ask for help—and see how your company grows as a result.

[SPY MYTHS DECODED]

YOU CAN START A CAREER IN THE CIA AT PRACTICALLY ANY AGE.

True!

You do not have to apply to the CIA immediately after graduation to be considered for a career as an intelligence officer. Many people who work for the CIA have had long and successful careers in other areas. Many of my colleagues have enjoyed careers in different branches of the military before working as intelligence officers. Law enforcement is also a popular first career before joining the CIA. Ultimately, the CIA needs people from so many different backgrounds and skills that applicants are not limited to new college grads. The CIA requires a bachelor's degree, but it looks for people who have studied everything from business and international relations to economics, finance, and chemical engineering. The group of people assembled at headquarters is incredibly diverse because protecting America requires appreciation for people with different skill sets, backgrounds, personalities, and life experiences.

CHAPTER 11

ACTIVE AWARENESS

The Simple Tactic That Can
Transform Your Business

Some of the simplest concepts in life often hold the most power. This is absolutely true when it comes to intelligence training. People often ask me, "What's the most valuable piece of information you learned in your training?" It's true that I'm well versed in self-defense moves, and I'm confident I could defend myself against most people (although my training has also taught me to always do everything I can to avoid a physical confrontation). I also admit I do have some James Bond–worthy skills: I could follow just about anyone and they'd have no idea I was doing it.

But the most valuable lessons I've learned aren't sexy—they're not even the least bit exciting, and you'll never see them in a James Bond or Jason Bourne movie. But a failure to follow these tactics is what gets people killed in an emergency and causes businesses to fail. Early on in our training as intelligence officers we learn about two key concepts, and both of them have changed my life.

SITUATIONAL AWARENESS:
The Number-One Thing That Can Keep You Safe

If there's one thing I could teach absolutely everyone to practice, it would be situational awareness. People who receive my survival newsletter have heard me speak of this before.

Situational awareness is the way in which we maneuver through the world in an alert and engaged manner. Sounds easy, right? Not necessarily if you have a habit of always looking at your phone, texting while you're walking, making calls while driving, playing video games on public transportation, and generally walking through the streets of your city or hometown with blinders on. One of the greatest differences between an intelligence officer and your average civilian is that the average person is trying to drown out his immediate surroundings. An intelligence officer is not going to put on headphones and listen to his favorite playlist so he can eliminate all the noise from the street. The sounds and signals that are reverberating through society act as signals to an intelligence officer that all is well . . . *or not*. Have you ever been watching the news when a witness is talking about an accident and says, "The car came out of nowhere!" Truth is, though, that everything comes from somewhere. Intelligence officers are taught to be constantly assessing an environment so that we're alert and ready when something does happen.

GET OFF THE X:
What to Do Immediately When Something Happens

The other concept that's drilled into us early on in our training is to "get off the X." The X is the hot zone, it's the place where something dangerous and potentially lethal is going down. The only way to save yourself in such a situation—be it a shooting or a natural disaster—is to move. And move immediately. If you're thinking, *Well of course, that's exactly what I'd do in an emergency,* please know that you have your own human nature battling against you, and it's battling hard. It's incredibly common for people to freeze when faced with a life-threatening situation. In my first book, *Spy Secrets That Can Save Your Life,* I talked about how the biggest danger from a plane disaster is from fire, not from a crash. I recounted the tragic story of a woman and her husband who survived a terrible fire on a plane because they were able to force themselves to get up and move. They could not rouse their good friend to move, and she unfortunately perished. Our instinct to freeze when faced with danger is strong, and it can be harder to reverse this than you think.

THE PRACTICE OF ACTIVE AWARENESS:
The Greatest Gift My Intelligence Training Has Given Me

Like many of you who started businesses, I was immediately faced with what felt like hundreds of choices to make. There were decisions about branding, computer equipment, software, supplies, shipping services, whether or not to hire staff, whom to hire . . . the list went on and on. It's a lot of work, and it's easy to feel overwhelmed and bogged down by all the details. While I was chipping away at what felt like the longest to-do list in history, the rest of the world kept moving forward as usual. Other companies were being launched, survival and security conferences were taking place, and people were facing new cyber security threats and scams daily.

From day one in the CIA, I had been taught about situational awareness. I knew that this concept was more likely to save my life than any of my firearms or self-defense skills. Now that I was responsible for my own income, I'd need to be aware of what was going on in the area of survival and self-defense. This sounds self-evident, but every businessperson knows that you have to keep a pulse on the competition. Situational awareness isn't about being hyperaware, though; it's about mastering a particular kind of awareness. In the intelligence world, this is called code yellow. Code yellow means you're aware of what's going on but not overanalyzing everything to the point that you can't function. (Code orange is the level of hyperawareness, and it has its time and place.) If I could operate in code yellow when it came to my business, I'd be able to focus on what I really needed to know and not let myself be bogged down by too much information. Getting off the X was also something I deeply understood. If someone is running at me with a sharp knife, the only way I cease being his target is by moving. As I was sitting at my desk surrounded by piles of papers and notes, I suddenly understood that if I wasn't careful, I wasn't going to get off the X. The papers, to-do lists, forms, and files represented something that could take me down if it got too out of control. I realized that getting off the X meant being deliberate and swift with my decision making. Getting off the X meant that I would not suffer from analysis paralysis, which is so easy to do in the age of easy information. With information about absolutely everything at our fingertips, it's easy to get lost in a vortex of research, reviews, articles, and studies. The tactics I took from my training have helped me streamline, move forward, and run a lean and successful business. Practicing active awareness will help you stay focused, predict events, and remain connected to your team members. Following are some easy ways to start practicing active awareness.

SEPARATE IMMEDIATE-ACTION PROJECTS FROM LONG-TERM PROJECTS

I make a point to avoid analysis paralysis whenever possible. While some decisions require more thought and planning than others, entrepreneurs can easily get bogged down in the decision-making process. In the intelligence world, if you stay on the X, you die. You must move, just as in business decisions must be made and then executed. At Spy Escape & Evasion, I separate immediate-action projects from long-term projects. I've decided that when it comes to immediate-action projects, a decision will be made within twenty-four hours. Examples of things that fall into this category might be a new design for a newsletter, an idea for an article, or transportation arrangements for a private client flying in for training. Long-term projects may include new shipping procedures, an idea for a webinar, or a concept for a new book. Only you yourself can know when you start to feel stifled by the decision-making process. Decide which items can be taken off your plate by a quick decision and which require more attention. Predetermine a time frame for immediate-action projects. Give yourself enough time so that you are making a smart decision but not enough that you can overanalyze, ultimately creating bigger problems. Watch how dividing your decision-making process in this simple fashion makes life easier, gets things done faster, and removes stress.

What/who are your go-to sources? While it's crucial to keep an eye on the competition and the various developments taking place in your industry, it's not necessary to keep tabs on everything to stay relevant. Create a focus base for assessment and stick to it. Choose the events, companies, players, and publications that will provide you with the most valuable and useful information and focus on those. A spy isn't going to run around town asking three dozen people what they think is going on—he determines who are his best sources and then maximizes the information he gets from them.

Know the baseline of your own business: It's essential that you are aware of the baseline of your own business. This may include the approximate amount of income you're bringing in each month, the expenses going out, the incoming orders for particular projects, and the timing of work being completed by your employees. Large corporations have software for tracking everything and analysts on staff to keep tabs on what's going on. Knowing the baseline of your business can serve the same function. Expenses getting out of control? Maybe you need to change vendors or talk to your employees about expenses. If you're a smaller operation like me, knowing the baseline can alert you to potential problems before they become actual problems.

[SPY MYTHS DECODED]

ONLY A VERY SELECT HANDFUL OF PEOPLE
ARE PRIVY TO GOVERNMENT SECRETS.

False!

When I refer to my colleagues throughout this book, it's easy to assume that everyone can be lumped into one category (spies). Ultimately, that's not quite true. There are so many different branches of intelligence, and even more levels of security clearance. Over 5 million people in the United States have security clearance and are given access to sensitive materials. Nearly 1.5 million people have clearance to look at "top-secret" materials. It seems like "top-secret" would include all of our nation's most valuable secrets, but the truth is that there are several levels of security clearance above and beyond "top-secret." Some of these security levels are so elite that I can't even tell you what they're called. No kidding.

CHAPTER 12

ELIMINATE, DON'T ACCUMULATE

How to Run a Successful Operation with Less

One does not accumulate, but eliminate. It is not daily increase but daily decrease. The height of cultivation always runs to simplicity.

—BRUCE LEE

When I was first starting out as an entrepreneur, I joined the local chamber of commerce (for networking purposes and opportunities to book paid speaking engagements), and I forked out money to be part of two "mastermind" groups (expensive, but worth it). The dollars I've made thanks to the connections at these events more than paid for the fees, but perhaps the most helpful souvenir has been a brilliant piece of advice I heard several times but that took some time to resonate with me: *Watch your expenses as you scale and watch your overhead.*

It's common for entrepreneurs to follow a certain "entrepreneurial life cycle." When first starting a business, you are doing almost everything yourself. You're most likely using your own money to finance your company—money you may not even be sure you have—and you're working *all the time*. As your business starts to grow, you're able to hire an employee or two to lighten the load. Now that you have more hands on deck, things can really take off. Orders fly in, the phone keeps ringing, and your customer base grows. Before you know it, your team of one or two expands to a dozen, plus a brand-new space.

All of this seems crucial to your company's survival, but it is also expensive. As your business continues to thrive and the money rolls in, some major headaches are coming your way. And these headaches are growing pains that indicate you've reached the part of the entrepreneurial life cycle where things get tough. The staff, office space, resources—all of it equals major overhead. Suddenly, you find yourself thinking about getting bigger just to be able to support how big you've already grown (there's a paradox for you). Meanwhile, your biggest challenges have shifted. No longer are you worried about finding a customer or figuring out how to produce a new product—you're stressed with decisions about employee benefits and warehouse repairs. This isn't the lifestyle you've envisioned. You want the income minus the headaches and problems.

I'm writing this book from my office in my home. My commute takes about ten seconds, and if I'm not appearing on TV or speaking at a conference, I'm not going to bother putting on a suit and tie. My wife and kids are right upstairs. It's a good life. I've also managed to make millions of dollars selling safety and survival items, books, and courses online—all things I believe in passionately. But the real winner for me is that I have cracked the code for doing all of this in as stress-free and efficient a manner as possible. I took stock of how the company was running and actually slashed $40,000 in expenses *per month*.

As Spy Escape & Evasion moved through its life cycle, I didn't just hire employees and rent a warehouse where we were packing and shipping all of the products—I bought an office building. In no time at all, my business became unnecessarily expensive to run. As things moved forward, my team grew. Eventually it became clear that while most of my employees were stellar, there were a few who weren't up to par and had to go. Instead of brainstorming about new products or pitching television shows to develop more business, I was dealing with workers' compensation and repairs on that office building. None of this was overwhelmingly huge, but my company was being weighed down by excess. When a spy is out on a mission, it's crucial he has everything he needs to accomplish his mission—whether that's a high-powered telescope or an armored vehicle disguised as a typical minivan. There are certain things he'll have in ample supply—water, matches, ammunition. Everything else is a burden. Every other item is something that has to be carried, watched out for, or left behind if he has to flee. Spies slash through the extras and get down to the most essential basics. Why was I doing the opposite with my own company? I realized I needed to take a long hard look at what I *actually* needed for my operation . . . and slash out the rest. When making choices about what I needed to maximize the chances of finishing my mission (in this case, running a successful, profitable company), I looked at the following:

Who are the core team members for this operation? There are some crucial members of my team who are the backbone of the operation. This is my customer service team, my marketing team, and my IT nerds. I appreciate all their hard work and I like making it clear they play a crucial role in the operation.

How can I utilize the freelance network? An amazing aspect of the technological age is that skilled work—from copywriting to packing and shipping—is a click or two away. I started contracting out projects. This has slashed my expenses but has also enabled me to connect with some fantastic freelancers whose skill I have truly come to value. If you're already using a freelancer but your workload is growing, or you need to connect with someone who has a specific area of expertise, use other freelancers to help you get to the next level.

What kind of base do I really need? Putting my office building on the market and selling it has made life significantly easier all around. Now all our orders are processed out of a fulfillment center. I no longer have to deal with the headaches of a warehouse. If I need a meeting room for an event or company meeting, I can easily rent one.

When all was said and done, I realized that I had managed to slash $40,000 in monthly expenses. That's not just money—it's my time and it's my quality of life. As you're building your business, think about what you *really* need. I'm not suggesting that you take on the entire load yourself, but be honest about what's essential to make your operation run smoothly and in a profitable manner. When spies are out on a mission, extra items aren't viewed as luxuries but as burdens. It can be tough to tell the difference between the two at times: Is this element of my business crucial, or do I just believe it's making my life easier? That great Bruce Lee quote that launched this chapter? I keep that message right on my desk as a constant reminder that less is more. Less means fewer expenses, fewer complications—but more time to spend with the people who mean the most to me. And, as you know, those people are right upstairs.

PART THREE

Protecting Your Most Important Asset

Spy-Level Deception Detection and Security Measures

Safety and security are two of my biggest concerns in life, and I work hard to stay up to date on the biggest threats facing your average American today. I do this because I don't believe in living with fear. I believe in empowering myself and others with information, knowledge, and skills. If you're anything like me, you've worked hard to build your company from the ground up. You value your freedom and you're over-seeing your own career. I want to help you protect one of your most important assets: your company.

As such, it's crucial to learn the difference between someone you can trust and someone who is best avoided. And also, while technology has given us many wonderful freedoms (such as the ability to keep in touch while traveling, answer your email in your pajamas, or send messages from the beach), it also has a dangerous flip side. It seems like every time you turn on the news you hear of yet another data breach or scam. Technology is a crucial component to running any business today, but if done correctly (and safely), you can continue to enjoy working at your favorite coffee shop without having to worry about a security breach.

CHAPTER 13

THE INTEGRITY TEST

How to Fill Your Team with Honest People

We've all read these stories in the paper or seen them on the evening news: A nanny is caught abusing a child in her charge, an accountant at a small firm embezzles hundreds of thousands of dollars, an employee steals thousands of dollars worth of merchandise from the store where he works. Despite the onslaught of such bad news, it is my true belief that 99 percent of people are good, decent, and honest human beings—and those are the kinds of people with whom I want to work. And I'm lucky I have the skills to ensure that I hire honest, hardworking people. It will probably come as no surprise that intelligence officers are human lie detectors, well versed in the art of deception detection. While there are specialists in my field who have spent a lifetime studying and perfecting their expertise in this area, just knowing some of the most basic concepts about deception can help you avoid hiring a thief or dishonest person. On the flip side, knowing how to avoid common behaviors that send a small signal that you're being deceptive can also help you get hired more quickly as well as make stronger business connections. When building my team and deciding with whom I want to work, I follow these rules:

RULE #1:
ASSESS THE FIRST THREE TO FIVE SECONDS

During an interview in which you've already had an in-depth conversation about an applicant's previous experience and work history and the conversation is flowing well, all signs point to a likely match . . . except for one thing: How do you know you can really trust this person? I will admit that I've been in interviews with people who seem great, but then I drop the crucial question and I know instantly that I can't hire them. The first three to five seconds after I ask the crucial question are key. Why? It's simple: Human beings are terrible liars. That's why I ask every person whom I am considering bringing onto my team the same thing:

"Tell me about the last time you stole something."

The phrasing of the question is deliberate. I don't say "Have you ever stolen anything?" It's "Tell me about the last time you stole something." This is the same phrasing the government uses to vet potential recruits. They sit us down and say, "Tell me about the last time you did drugs." They assume everyone has done something stupid like smoke pot in college. Phrasing the question as an assumption puts the interviewee in a position of having to address the issue directly.

The reaction is as important as the answer. Most people will display honesty and integrity by answering right away. Typical responses have included everything from "I stole a Snickers bar from the grocery store when I was ten" to "I walked out of the library with a book in my backpack when I was in grade school." Everyone has stolen something at some point in their lives, even if it was just an extra lollipop from the candy bowl at the doctor's office. It's normal for kids to push limits, but they quickly learn that it is wrong to do so. If someone answers quickly and honestly that they stole a candy bar, I'm fine with it because that is normal, and it doesn't shoot up any red flags. However, there are responses that sound my internal alarm right away, including:

Fidgeting and discomfort

Stuttering

Periods of silence

Blank stares

Once again, because we are terrible liars, our brain must work hard to come up with a response. People who exhibit the above responses are generally thinking about what they can say that will make them sound like loyal applicants who should get the job. I once interviewed a woman who seemed uncomfortable right away when I asked this question, her facial expression the very definition of "deer in the headlights." As usual, I let her know that everyone has stolen something at some point in their lives. "It's normal and okay," I said. "We all do stupid things." Upon prodding her, the woman sat up straighter and proceeded to explain that she stole a bunch of office supplies from her previous company. But she went on. It turned out it wasn't a handful of paper clips or a few pens; she was planning on starting a competing business and wanted to give herself a head start in the supply department. I immediately knew I wasn't giving her the job. That she thought it was okay to do something like this as an adult was telling, but that she was comfortable doing this and sharing it with a potential employer was another.

RULE #2: THE HEAD NOD NEVER LIES

The head nod is so accurate it can almost be comical. Intelligence officers who have training in deception detection will notice this move all the time—and sometimes we can't help but laugh. Our heads tell the truth, always. If you were to discover upon opening your cookie jar that it was devoid of cookies, you could ask your kid if they ate them, and while they could say no (even though their face was probably covered in crumbs), their head will be vehemently nodding yes. I guarantee you that you've seen this phenomenon in the media. If Hillary Clinton is asked about her marriage, she'll respond that she and Bill have a good marriage, but it isn't hard to notice that her head is moving in the negative direction. The same with former senator John Edwards. When explaining he'd be happy to take a paternity test back in 2008, his head was clearly shaking no. If a potential employee is explaining they've never faced a challenge with a co-worker but their head is nodding yes, they're giving you their answer—just not verbally. Body language experts will tell you that the motion of the head should match the words. If an individual is saying "No, I've never been arrested" but their head is nodding gently up and down, chances are they aren't telling the truth.

RULE #3: WATCH FOR THE THREE FAILURES

Failure to use spatial references and sensory terms when telling a story are a significant indicator that the person is being deceitful. If they're telling a story about a negotiation they valiantly saved but don't use special sensory terms in their description, take caution. Examples could be along the lines of "I felt great. I had been so nervous the deal wasn't going to go through," or "The walk to the conference room was long, it felt like it took forever to get there." Those comments indicate truthfulness. Another failure to watch out for? Liars don't use contractions, they'll use a full phrase to create a sense of emphasis. A famous example is provided by Bill Clinton, who said, "I did not have sex with that woman." Not "didn't" but "did not." When Sheryl Sandberg was interviewed on PBS about Facebook's massive data breach, Sandberg nodded her head in the affirmative when she said, "We didn't do a good job," indicating she genuinely felt this way.

RULE #4: NOTE BRIDGE TERMS

Bridge terms are like gap fillers. They are phrases a dishonest person may resort to if they're trying to cover up the real story. These are typical phrases that often have the effect of signaling a tall tale. If someone is peppering a story with the following bridge phrases, be sure to take caution:

> *"And then . . ."*
>
> *"And then I/she/he/we did . . ."*
>
> *"I did this next . . ."*

"The next thing I know . . ."

"Before I knew what was happening . . ."

"What happened next was . . ."

"Suddenly . . ."

These four rules can help weed out a bad egg, but you must be diligent in other areas too. I am constantly shocked how reluctant people are to do a background check on potential employees. It's not terribly hard or expensive to do, and it can save you a tremendous amount of trouble down the road. You company is your biggest asset, so make it a point to do everything you can to ensure you're hiring the best and brightest.

[SPY SKILLS TAKEAWAY]

USE INDIRECT QUESTIONING TO DIG INTO THE MINDS OF POTENTIAL EMPLOYEES

Spies certainly aren't the only people who use unusual questions to glean what's going on inside someone's head. More and more often, companies are using indirect questioning methods to learn additional information about job candidates. This method involves inferring information about skills, knowledge, values, and problem-solving abilities by noting the answers to the questions. As an intelligence officer, I have found this practice easy to use and very useful. I've put together our favorite indirect questions that we like to use at Spy Escape & Evasion.

SPY ESCAPE & EVASION

INDIRECT QUESTIONING FOR POTENTIAL CANDIDATES.

To assess general personality:
"What is your favorite color?"
> *Red is typically aggressive or confrontational.*
> *Blue or green suggests a mild temperament.*

To assess ability to lead, organize, and evaluate:
"How would you wrangle a heard of cats?"

To assess problem-solving abilities:
"If you were trapped in a blender, what would you do to get out?"

To assess ability to overcome challenges:
"Define Jell-O without using the word *gelatin*."

To assess optimism, or an openness to possibility:
"Do you believe in life on other planets?"

To assess general honesty (note pauses or nervousness before answering):
"Tell me about the last time you stole something."

To assess how a person evaluates organizational changes:
"If you were CEO of your last company, what would you have changed?"

To assess a person's awareness of their personal value and key skills:
"If you were a share of stock, why should someone buy you?"

[SPY MYTHS DECODED]

SPIES ARE USUALLY FOUND HANGING AROUND DIVE BARS AND OTHER SEEDY ESTABLISHMENTS.

False!

Well, almost. Spies generally will do whatever it takes to find the right assets, and if that means hanging out in a seedy bar, then that's what they'll do. However, there's one very interesting place in which it wouldn't be uncommon to find a spy: your local bookstore. Believe it or not, during training, spies often use a bookstore as a starting base for operations. The reason is that a bookstore is a place where people can quietly hang out and browse without anyone being suspicious. A bookstore is usually full of people quietly browsing books. Ultimately, it's the perfect place in which to stick a bunch of spies in training. They can hang out with zero suspicions while awaiting further instructions about their next move.

CHAPTER 14

CYBER SECURITY

Easy Ways to Stay Safe

One of the key elements of operating a business that many people don't like to think about is cyber security. It's easy to push it aside and decide to deal with it tomorrow or, sadly, not at all. Suddenly, a security breach occurs and you're wishing you had protected yourself.

Cyber security matters whether you're running a software company or a knitting shop. Everyone is a potential target. It's not the most fun part of running a business, but not paying attention to how you handle these matters can be devastating. In order to keep your company and yourself safe, consider these items:

ITEM #1 BEWARE OF THE USB

When President Trump met with Korea's Kim Jong-un in Singapore, the temperatures soared. It was *hot* in Singapore. Journalists covering the summit each received an interesting gift bag that contained water bottles, a handheld fan featuring the faces of Trump and Kim, and a miniature electric fan. To cool off, all you had to do was insert the fan into your computer's USB port. If this seems like a terrible idea, you are completely right. Think about it. A Chinese company had manufactured USB-powered fans that the government provided to reporters, what could go wrong?

The reality is that using USB devices is an extremely common method of gathering intelligence. If China altered these USB fans for spying purposes, it wouldn't have been the first time. According to a *Washington Post* report, "In 2008, Russian agents planted virus-carrying USB sticks in retail kiosks around NATO headquarters in Kabul, Afghanistan, to gain access to a classified Pentagon network." The frightening thing is that the countries that use USB devices to spy aren't just targeting other spies. They're also targeting average citizens like you and me. So, I wanted to share some basic precautions you should follow:

> **Don't trust unknown devices:** Never plug any type of USB device you didn't personally purchase or doesn't come from someone you know and trust into any of your personal devices. If you find some sort of USB device with the presidential seal on it or a giant sticker that reads TOP-SECRET INFORMATION, don't let your curiosity

get the best of you. Chances are you'll regret it when your
computer is infected with malware.

Purchase from reputable companies only: When buying USB
devices, make sure to purchase them from a reputable
company or manufacturer. I certainly don't recommend
buying one off Craigslist or eBay.

Don't share: Be careful using the same device on multiple
computers. Now, I realize the entire point of a thumb drive
is to be able to move files from one computer to another.
However, this is incredibly risky because you can cross-
contaminate your computers if the USB device happens to
be infected. For sharing files among different computers,
I recommend using cloud storage because the cloud
encrypts your information. Using a compromised flash
drive, charging cable, or mini fan on different computers
could infect all of them.

Use biometric authentication and strong passwords:
Depending on the device, some USBs can be set up to
require fingerprint authentication or a password. You
should absolutely use these options on any device you
can. This way if the device falls into the wrong hands, you
won't have to worry that someone will simply add malware
and give it back to you, putting your information at risk.

ITEM #2 BEWARE OF SMART HOME
AND OFFICE TECHNOLOGY

A thirty-one-year old Springfield, Missouri, man named Marcus decided to jump on the smart home bandwagon and change all of the devices in his house for more modern, high-tech versions. And I mean ALL. He didn't just change a light bulb or two. Marcus spent thousands of dollars on thirty Phillips LED light bulbs, two Ecobee thermostats, eight temperature sensors to put throughout his house, and an August Smart Lock for his front door. But then there was trouble in paradise. When designing his smart home ecosystem, Marcus chose devices that were compatible with the Apple Home-Kit. That way he could use his iPad as a voice-controlled base station for all his connected devices. For the first month, everything worked flawlessly. The lights in his home would gradually brighten after he woke up and he was able to unlock his front door as he approached.

Then one day, as Marcus was leaving for work, his neighbor stopped him in his driveway and asked if he could borrow a cup of flour. Of course, Marcus said, "Sure!" That's when things went south. Marcus watched as his neighbor simply walked up to his front door and said, "Hey, Siri, unlock the front door." Marcus's front door unlocked. After the initial shock, Marcus tried doing the same thing multiple times to see if it was a one-time fluke or if it was truly that simple for someone else to get into his house. Unfortunately, each time he tried to unlock the door, it opened easily. The problem was that Marcus's iPad was in his living room not far from the front door. The iPad could hear the neighbor's command and it unlocked the door for him. The next day Marcus removed the smart door lock.

THE HUMAN FACTOR

To be clear, this problem was not caused by a security flaw with the iPad or the August Smart Lock. It happened because Marcus didn't require a password on his iPad. If there had been a password, he would have had to physically go over to the iPad, enter the password, and then say, "Hey, Siri, unlock the front door." Marcus admitted he didn't do this because enabling a password would defeat the purpose of having smart technology in his home. The whole point was to be able to control things without having to physically do anything.

The fact is that many homes and offices these days are being equipped with smart technology. However, one of the biggest security risks when buying, selling, or even renting a home or office space these days is the vulnerability of this technology: what information you are exposing and if people can use it to get into your home or your office (or both if you work at home like I often do). Here are three things to consider whether you are buying, selling, or renting a home or office space with any piece of so-called smart equipment:

Inventory the devices. The first thing you should do when buying a new home or renting an office is inventory the smart technology devices currently installed. Decide what you want to keep and what you want to get rid of and immediately disable any devices you don't want.

Remove old profiles. Most smart devices have a user profile that contains a log of the user's information and habits. For instance, most security systems record when you come and go, which could reveal your work schedule or daily habits to a potential criminal. Also, if there is a monthly fee associated with any of your devices, call the monitoring company and ask them to remove your payment information when you sell the house. Don't forget to submit the required documents showing a change of property ownership.

Update and reset. Whether you are moving in or moving out, update and restore all smart devices to their factory settings. Be sure to change all system passwords and user names upon taking possession of a new home. If possible, create unique passwords and user names for administrative accounts that are different from the everyday log-ins. Last, reset access and guest codes for home alarm systems, gates, and garage door openers. The last thing you want is to end up like Marcus where anyone could enter your home for a cup of flour—or something more.

Personally, I don't have any smart devices in my home, which is also where I do a lot of my work. They're just too easy to hack at this point. It's a risk to my home and my business. And if the power goes out (or the entire grid goes down), I still want to be able to get in my front door and I don't want my business to be compromised. Imagine not being able to issue commands to your home because your iPad is dead and you can't charge it. In other words, I like to keep things simple and unlock my door the good old-fashioned way. Whatever you decide is right for your home and workplace, just be sure to be careful.

ITEM #3 BEWARE OF USING THE TRUTH WHEN SETTING UP NEW ACCOUNTS

You're shopping online and find the perfect anniversary present for your wife. It's a beautiful, handmade necklace sold by a mid-sized national jewelry manufacturer. You happily put it in your cart and start typing in the information to make your purchase. You're asked to set up an account and you start adding your address, email, phone number, et cetera. Then come the typical security questions, like "What is your mother's maiden name?" That's when you should stop. Get ready to lie like a rug. How many times have you set up an online account and been asked pertinent information such as your birth date or mother's maiden name? If you're asked for this information when creating a new account—make it up! Just be sure to make up something you will remember if you ever need to recover your password.

The reason you should lie is that these details are easy to figure out using social media (this is also the reason you should be wary of what you post). Let's say you post a picture of your mother. From there a hacker would be able to look at your mother's social media accounts and they could easily find out her maiden name. Ultimately, you shouldn't even use your name when you create an account. Instead, use another word you will remember, such as "Hawaii" or "peanut." The fact is, a harmless social media post about a family reunion could turn into a big mess if the wrong person sees it and does a little bit of digging.

ALWAYS GO BACK TO BASICS

Don't recycle: One of the best things you can do to keep your information safe is to use good passwords. Never reuse a password on multiple websites and be sure to regularly change your passwords on ALL of your accounts.

Say yes to two-factor: In addition, always enable two-factor authentication for logging into websites. This will require you to use another form of identification—such as entering a code sent to you by text message or email—as well as the password you created.

Use a manager: Another option to consider is using a password manager, such as LastPass. This will help you securely store all your different passwords for your online accounts.

Cyber attacks are easy to get away with and difficult to stop, which means they're only going to increase. The thing is, cyber crimes are simply a numbers game. Hackers know that if they contact a large number of people, someone at some point will always take the bait. That's the reason so many hackers are so successful and rarely get caught. The more you can do to secure your online accounts, the better. If you make it tough for hackers to penetrate your accounts and collect critical information, the more likely they are to move on to another target who isn't as secure.

ITEM #4 BE AWARE THAT OTHERS ARE LIKELY LISTENING IN ON YOUR PRIVATE PHONE CALLS

Currently, an estimated 6 million people call the Washington, D.C., metropolitan area home. With a population of that size, it's easy for people (and things) to blend in. Let's say someone left a small item the size of a suitcase in an alley or under a stairwell. It would likely go unnoticed for a while. Well, that's exactly what's happening *around* our nation's capital. Now, these aren't just empty suitcases or bags belonging to homeless people. They aren't homemade explosives either—thank goodness. They are small electronic gadgets designed to mimic a cellphone tower. In other words, these devices trick your phone into connecting to it instead of an actual cellphone tower, thus intercepting your phone call.

SOMEONE IS LISTENING

According to the Department of Homeland Security (DHS), these spying devices are a growing risk. They have been found in several high-profile areas, including near the Trump Hotel on Pennsylvania Avenue. The DHS warns that these devices could prevent cellphones from making 911 calls as well as intercept calls and messages. Even worse, authorities have confessed they haven't determined who is operating them. Most likely, these devices are being deployed by foreign governments. Most U.S. government officials believe it to be either China or Russia. The bottom line is that we know that our cellphone communications are easily listened in on and that a massive amount of data is constantly being collected. In fact, I was recently talking to a former agency colleague who told me he assumes every phone call he makes is being monitored—and he's probably right. That's why I want to introduce you to three different smartphone applications that can encrypt your phone calls. For the sake of your privacy and security, I recommend using them—no matter where you live.

1. **Silent Phone:** This app is available for both iOS and Android and is free for most users. Silent Phone protects calls, video chat, and messaging with end-to-end encryption (as long as both people are using the app). Silent Phone does allow communication with nonusers, but you will be secure on your end at the very least. In addition, you can securely send PDF, DOCX, MOV, MP4, PNG, and JPEG files, which is a great feature if you want to keep your business dealings private. You can even do encrypted conference calling, so if you wanted all your employees on a secure call together, this would be the best app for you.

2. **Signal:** This is another free application for iOS and Android phones. It also uses end-to-end encryption, which means the server never has access to any of your communications and does not store any of your data. One of the best things about this app is that it allows you to use your same cellphone number—it doesn't require you to create separate log-ins, usernames, passwords, or PINs to use the app. For those who are tech experts, this app is open source—anyone can verify its security protocol to make sure it's top notch. Another beneficial feature of this app is that you can create fully encrypted group chats. The app never has

access to the group's metadata, so the company can't identify who joined the group chat.

3. **Apple FaceTime:** This application is exclusive to Apple products, but it's free and available for use on iPhones, iPads, and Mac laptops and desktops. Apple has no way to decrypt FaceTime data when it's in transit between devices, so unlike other companies' messaging services, Apple can't scan your communications. Even if a federal court ordered Apple to produce communications between people on FaceTime, the company wouldn't be able to do so simply because it doesn't store that information. There is no question Apple is one of the leading tech companies when it comes to protecting the security of its users.

In this day and age, I would tell every American to act like there is always someone listening in on their phone conversations. With the spying that goes on these days, everyone is at risk—even if you aren't a clandestine government employee.

I believe in empowerment. I believe in self-reliance. The truth is, we all have areas of our lives where we need more help than others. It's been my experience that some entrepreneurs are reluctant to dig in and take care of their own cyber security. I hope this primer has shown you that some of the most basic and most important cyber security measures you can take for your company are easy to implement. You've worked hard to build your dream company, and you deserve it to be protected and safe from harm.

SELF-RELIANCE:
The Power Is in You

I'm grateful every day that I had the opportunity to work as an intelligence officer on behalf of the United States. I'm also in the unique position to continue working with former intelligence officers in my day-to-day work. I've shared many spy concepts with you, and I absolutely believe they will help you grow your business—but just remember that all of this boils down to one thing: You alone have the power to create, build, and grow the business you've always dreamed about. Spies in the field are the most self-reliant people out there. A deep commitment to self-reliance is what will keep your business moving ahead and thriving, even when facing obstacles that make doing so feel impossible. Intelligence officers face unimaginable situations, and in those dark moments the one thing they can always tap into is their self-reliance. You too must believe that you are capable and possess the right skills and experience to take care of yourself and survive at any moment.

I know that running a business can feel like climbing a mountain; it's about putting one foot in front of the other, and often it feels like the journey will never end. Sometimes the climb gets easier, and you can even take a moment to stop and enjoy the view. And then it gets tough again. Those difficult moments are when we grow the most. They're when we discover a new way to tackle a problem or find that we're ready to embark on a new venture. As you're moving forward, one step after the other, just remember that the power is in you. Self-reliance will give you the strength to get to that next positive place every time.

The Ultimate Primer for Transforming Yourself into a Media Personality to Earn a Small Fortune for Your Business

Rather than ask me about my deep dark secrets from my time in the CIA (I'd never tell anyway), what people always want to know is this: "How did you manage to get on TV? And how can I do it?" There's no denying it, we live in a celebrity-obsessed culture. People who write books, for magazines, and newspapers or who are featured on TV are viewed as the foremost experts in their areas (even though that may not always be the case). People *trust* the people they see on TV. As someone who values privacy and who has never even had a pizza delivered to my home, I wasn't exactly excited about the idea of appearing on TV in front of thousands and, later, millions of people. The truth is, while my career in the CIA had prepared me for many things, when it came to television and other forms of media, I had absolutely no idea what I was doing. I didn't have a single useful connection in the TV world. That being said, I knew that creating a media presence for myself would be an enormous boost for my brand (and it was free) if only I could figure out a way in. I ultimately decided that the pros outweighed the cons. The pros included free advertising for my company, massive exposure, and a huge opportunity to feature my products and present myself as an expert; the cons, as far as I could tell, were limited to me looking like an idiot in front of lots of people. I decided I would methodically do everything I could to crack the code and get myself on TV. I'm pleased to say that I managed to pull it off, and it has helped my business tremendously and I now help others do the same through my marketing company at www.SpymasterBook.com. I have appeared on over thirty television shows, including those with national audiences such as NBC's *Today Show, Good Morning America, Dateline, Fox & Friends,* and ABC's *Shark Tank.* And I've been a regular guest on shows hosted by Rachael Ray and Harry Connick Jr. I know I've said this a couple of times throughout this book, but it can't be emphasized enough: If I can do this, anyone can.

COMBAT BREATHING RELIEVES STRESS AND ANXIETY

I prepare like crazy for television appearances, and this makes me feel confident that the appearance will go well. However, for many people, there is nothing more unnerving than going on live television. Soldiers out in the field use a technique called combat breathing to manage stress. Combat breathing helps a person remain calm when adrenaline is flowing through the body. The technique works as follows:

1. Breathe in through your nose for a count of four.
2. Hold your breath for a count of four.
3. Exhale through your mouth for a count of four.
4. Hold your breath for a count of four.

This is also known as box breathing, because you can visualize the four sides of a box with each step. Repeat this cycle as many times as needed.

CAREFULLY BUILD YOUR CASE

I can be a very determined person, but I knew it would be a mistake to just randomly start calling producers and asking them to put me on TV. Instead, I decided to create a strong case for why I should be featured on television. I started to think hard about what I could offer and why someone should put me on the air by asking myself the following:

> What is unique about my business?
> What do I do that no one else does in my niche?
> What am I known for?
> What do friends and family find most interesting about my work?
> Why do companies hire me versus other companies?
> Why am I the best at what I do?

> › What credentials do I have that are completely unique?
> › How could I demonstrate my skills on television?
> › What could I do that was memorable?

Although my life as a former CIA officer gave me clout, it was hardly enough to get me booked on a show. There are plenty of other former CIA officers out there. But when I started pondering my niche and what my friends and family find most interesting about my work, something specific occurred to me. One of the things I teach people who hire me for security purposes is how to easily escape from duct tape. The number-one method used by criminals and kidnappers to abduct people is to tape their hands together with duct tape, because duct tape is readily available, inexpensive, and it seems nearly impossible to get out of. The fact is, it's incredibly easy to break free from duct tape, and I've routinely shown people how to escape if their wrists and ankles are taped, or even how to get out if they're bound to a chair. People were amazed whenever I demonstrated this. It's simple, anyone can do it, it's quick—and it results in the same jaw-dropping reaction every single time. At that moment, I realized that the jaw-dropper was my ticket to getting on TV.

ESTABLISH YOUR JAW-DROPPER

I didn't invent the duct tape escape, but I *did* show the American people how easy it is if you know how to do it. It's a very empowering skill that I've taught to children and eighty-three-year-old grandfathers, and I've now done it countless times on television segments all over the country. My jaw-dropper is what got me booked on all of these shows.

Now, I can guess what you're thinking. You don't have a duct tape escape or anything like it. That doesn't matter. Everyone has a unique process, methodology, trick, demonstration, tool, or formula that can turn them into a celebrity. I have coached many people through this process and I have never worked with a business where we couldn't come up with something that would not be exciting enough for TV. Joy Mangano, who is estimated to be worth $50 billion and whose life story was turned into a feature film, got her start on television mopping floors. Does anything sound more boring? But she knew that when she demonstrated how to wring out a mop she invented without touching dirty water, people would react. That was her jaw-dropping moment, and it's made her incredibly rich. Krazy Glue famously demonstrated its strength by gluing a construction worker's helmet to a steel girder to show how it could easily hold up the weight of a grown man. The superiority of Ginsu knives was shown to consumers when they saw how easily the blades could cut through a tin can.

While some of these stunts are dramatic, the jaw-dropper isn't necessarily about shocking people—it's about showing a unique property, of which people may not be aware, that has the power to improve their lives.

CHARACTERISTICS OF A GOOD JAW-DROPPER

› It's visual and involves some sort of demonstration. TV shows do not want a talking head. You and I are not George Clooney or Angelina Jolie—A List celebrities who can go on TV and just talk and that's pretty much it. Ordinary people like you and me must wow them with a visual demonstration.

> It's quick and can be executed in a fairly short amount of time. Segments on TV are a few minutes long at the most.

> It provides viewers with a solution to a problem or introduces them to an item that makes life more comfortable.

> It's not too difficult to execute; people at home need to feel that this is something they can do too.

> It's something you can do easily, every single time—it leaves little to no room for error. You don't want to attempt your jaw-dropper on TV only to realize you can't even get it started.

I was fortunate that the idea for my jaw-dropper was obvious. While it might take some real brainstorming to figure out yours, keep in mind that when you're an expert on something, it's easy to forget that you possess a skill that might seem like no big deal to you but it's extraordinary to other people. For instance, if you run a landscaping business, maybe you are often reviving a dead plant in the dead of winter. This is just day-to-day work for you, but to the rest of us who are terrible at gardening, it's very impressive. The beauty of the jaw-dropper is that it's not limited to any specific business. Hair stylists, pet groomers, landscapers, bakers, accountants, fitness coaches—every expert can share a tidbit of information in their own unique way and use it to blow people's minds.

**5 JAW-DROPPING SPY MOMENTS DURING
REAL CIA OPERATIONS**

1. Using the carcass of a dead animal to hide spy messages.
2. Placing double-stick tape on a car door to capture a drug kingpin's fingerprints.
3. Writing notes in a combustible notebook that is ignited when touched by a special pencil.
4. Bribing a food server to steal the dishes and cutlery used by an internationally wanted criminal to use for DNA testing.
5. Concealing your true identity by carrying fake brochures and business cards to appear like a regular, everyday person. Go ahead, call the phone number: It works.

PRACTICE, PRACTICE, AND PRACTICE AGAIN

Once you've figured out what your jaw-dropper is, practice it. Even though I had done the duct tape escape literally hundreds of times, I practiced like crazy. I wanted to make sure my approach made sense and that it was clear, easy to follow, and had just enough dramatic flair. I developed a concise explanation as to why this trick was important. I wanted a potential producer (and audience) to understand that this wasn't just a fun party trick (even though it is) but a potentially lifesaving technique that absolutely everyone should learn. Practice your jaw-dropper every chance you get—in front of a mirror, in front of your family, friends, strangers, anyone you can. Also make a point to think about what could go wrong and have a backup plan just in case. Every time I do this method on TV I have multiple rolls of tape ready to go. While, thankfully, not much can go wrong with this trick, I suppose it's possible I could drop the tape and it could roll off the stage. If this happened on live television I could just laugh it off, because I could whip another roll out of my bag in a second.

A WARNING: DON'T AGREE TO DO SOMETHING YOU MIGHT NOT BE ABLE TO DO JUST TO GET ON TV

Don't do anything you might not be able to deliver and prove you're a true expert. It may be tempting to go on a show and give it a try to get the TV exposure, but it's not worth it. I have appeared on the *Rachael Ray Show* over 10 times—and I am ever-grateful to Rachael and her producers—but on one occasion they reached out to me about showing people how to pick a lock on TV. They wanted me to demonstrate this by picking the lock on a filing cabinet. Now, I'm pretty darn good at picking locks and I can usually open a lock in less than thirty seconds (and on TV, thirty seconds is, strangely, a very long time). I know that things don't always go as planned when trying to pick a lock. For one reason or another, it might be a finicky lock and it might take you five attempts to open it. On national TV, you do not have time to fiddle with the lock multiple times—and you'll end up looking like the opposite of an expert. This isn't a position in which you ever want to be.

Against my better judgment, I agreed to go on the *Rachael Ray Show* and demonstrate how to pick a lock on a filing cabinet. Thankfully, I was able to pick the lock on my first try and the segment went great. I was greatly relieved because I knew it could've easily gone wrong. How embarrassing would it have been if I hadn't been able to pick the lock? What a terrible segment that few minutes would have been. What's worse, something like that is the kind of thing that can go viral—an expert ex-CIA officer is a failure at picking locks. What could be worse for my brand? I highly encourage you not to make the mistake I made and don't do any dangerous segments that might not work out for you.

HOW TO CRAFT THE PERFECT TV SEGMENT, AND MAKE MONEY DOING IT

So, you've practiced your jaw-dropper over and over, and you feel ready to pitch your segment to TV programs. Before you start reaching out to producers (and I'll share the best way to do that soon), I highly recommend you give yourself a big step up by crafting a good segment. It's great to have a skill that can blow people's minds, but you'll increase your chances of getting on TV if you build a good segment around it, creating context for your skill, and making sure that what you propose to do fits in with the show you're pitching. And if you're like me and you have bills to pay, you need to spin your segment in a manner that can help bring income to your company. After all, I love sharing my knowledge about survival and security— and I want to help people—but television appearances take up valuable time, and it only makes sense to do them in the context of your business if it brings you income. It always blows my mind when I'm sitting in the green room of some TV show and I chat with the other guests about why they're on the show.

Most of them are on TV to share knowledge and they're just happy to make an appearance; they have nothing to sell and don't anticipate making any income. While that's admirable, it doesn't make any sense. What these people don't understand is that their "fifteen minutes of fame" could be earning them thousands, tens of thousands, or even millions of dollars in revenue. Even if you work for a nonprofit, you should think about how you can spin this moment into a moneymaker for your organization. Do donors get a tote bag? A discount on tickets to an event? The bottom line is that anyone can offer a product or service as an incentive. I followed this simple multi-step process and have been on TV more times than I can count. If you want to earn more money and draw attention to your business by being on TV, I recommend you do the following:

Step 1: Research appropriate programs: It's crucial to know what shows would be a good match for your jaw-dropper. Which one has local people on frequently? Also important to note is how long segments generally are. Are multipart segments common? For example, Rachael Ray will often have me demonstrate one skill, then a second skill after a commercial break. Are the segments filmed in a studio or remotely? Do they ever do things on location? Can your jaw-dropping skill fit into their format? It's also a good idea to make note of segments that got your attention and may appeal to a similar audience. For example, if a station did a good segment on gun safety, which is a tenet I adhere to and promote, I'd note that. Keep a running list of segments that catch your interest.

Step 2: Establish the "why now": Why is what you have to demonstrate important to the show's audience right now?

Create a sense of urgency and relevancy when designing your segment. When I first pitched my duct tape escape, I made sure to put it into context for producers. I explained that this skill was potentially lifesaving because most kidnappers and criminals use this method to restrain their victims. I also pointed out that with the secret knowledge that I have, a child or elderly person could easily do it. Suddenly it seemed extremely important that everyone should have a handle on this easy-to-execute, potentially lifesaving skill.

Ask yourself:

> Why does everyone need to see my jaw-dropper right now?
> How can this skill change someone's life right now?

Remember, your skill doesn't have to change the course of history or even save someone's life. If you've figured out how to pack lunches that every kid will eat, even the extra-picky ones—that's going to make life easier for a lot of parents. It's about showing the value of your skill. Not seeing any segments that are in line with what you do? Then simply draw inspiration from how others present and pitch their skill. How are they relaying its importance? How do they create a sense of urgency? Which elements of their skill or products do they focus on?

Step 3: Make it visual: Television is a visual art form, and it's crucial that you adjust your jaw-dropping skill accordingly. If you own a chain of dry cleaners and have developed a stain removal method that works on anything, think through how this skill will look on TV. The audience needs to be able to see each step of the process. If the audience can't clearly see the ketchup stain on the shirt before and after you do your technique, no one will be wowed. Walk through your jaw-dropper again, this time asking yourself what the audience will be seeing. If it's not visual enough, make appropriate adjustments.

Step 4: Nail the timing: There is no room for error on a television show. Your segment must be timed perfectly, and you have to be able to execute your skill in the appropriate time frame over and over. A local news segment is going to be around three to four minutes in length and a national talk show might be eight to ten minutes. Since you're going to start on local TV, you need the segment you've crafted to be around four minutes long. Even though you may have done your demo several times (like I have done my duct tape escape in seminars and other events), you need to spend a lot of time practicing. When you get nervous it's possible you could fumble, and that will make things take longer—or you'll talk faster and fly through your presentation. Imagine how embarrassing it would be if you had four minutes for a segment and when your time was up you weren't even halfway done with your demonstration? Practice so that you're executing each moment of the demonstration the exact same way and at the exact same time.

Step 5: Put it all together: Once you've done your research, established your "why now," and worked out your timing, put it all together in a way that's comfortable for you. You might want to write out a script and practice it for your friends and family. Perhaps you want to record it so you can review it and make changes. Whatever method you chose, practice is key. The more you practice, the less nervous you'll be.

[PRO TIPS]

USE ANY HOLIDAY TO YOUR ADVANTAGE

Producers are always looking for segments that fit in with whatever holiday is coming up next. You can actually increase your chances of getting on television by creating holiday appropriate segments. For example, if it's the Christmas shopping season, I'd likely pitch a segment about how to stay safe in the mall parking lot. Whatever it is you're pushing, think about how you can tie it into a holiday. Is your landscaping service a perfect gift for dad? Pitch a segment about spring yard cleanup dos and don'ts. If you're a mechanic, pitch a segment about Labor Day car maintenance safety. Having a holiday tie-in is a great way to make your segment stand out from everyone else's. This is also a way for you to ease yourself into the national market.

THE UNEXPECTED QUESTION

Spies are trained to think quickly on their feet—so when they're presented with any unexpected questions they'll be able to come up with an appropriate answer. To get used to thinking quickly

and coming up with responses to questions you haven't anticipated, create your own focus group and do some market testing.
Perform your segment for as many friends, family members, and
co-workers as you can and tell them to ask you absolutely any
question they have—no matter how crazy. Doing this repeatedly
will likely result in your being asked more questions about your
service or product than you could have ever imagined. You'll be
ready to answer any questions thrown at you.

MASTER THE ART OF THE NON-SALE

Once you've created your segment, it's time to think about
how to sell it by *not* selling it at all. I know I just told you I
won't take the time to do a television appearance if I don't
have something to sell. While that's true, there's a difference
between selling something and *blatantly looking* like you're
selling something. The latter comes across as too self-serving
and as a turnoff. You must master the art of the non-sale.

I always make sure I'm incorporating the non-sale into my
segment. For example, one of our bestselling products is the
self-defense pen, aka the tactical pen. I have many testimonials from people whose lives have been saved by the tactical
pen. If my ultimate goal for the segment is to sell tactical pens,
I'll create a segment called something like "Five Little-Known
Self-Defense Tools That Will Keep Women Safe at Night." Or
maybe "The Number-One Self-Defense Tool for College Students." After I'm introduced as a former CIA officer and secu-

rity expert, I'll go into my segment, moving through the five self-defense tools women might want to carry. I'll purposely end with the tactical pen—demonstrating with urgency how important this pen can be should someone attack you. If I'm doing the college student segment, I might show how to use the tactical pen for self-defense, as well as how to use it to break out the window of a taxi or Uber should your driver be a maniac. (It can happen.)

At the end of the segment, the host will usually ask me where someone can get one of these pens, at which point I drop the name of my website. (We will use this segment in other ways to make money, and I will explain how to get even more bang for your buck later.) It is critical to remember that your segment must give people very valuable content. You can't come off as a snake-oil salesperson. That approach will backfire. Please note: I use this segment formula all of the time, and it has worked to sell everything from my books and tactical pens to flashlights and my Ultimate Spy Week training course.

GETTING TO YES:
How to Approach Producers and Get Yourself Booked on TV

You've found your jaw-dropper, you've crafted the perfect segment, you've practiced non-selling, and you can do the entire segment in exactly four minutes, even in your sleep. Now is the time to start approaching producers about appearing on the show. You might have the most jaw-dropping skill imaginable—but you're not going to start by calling producers at the *Today Show*. National shows are much harder to appear on, and while that's a great (and reasonable) goal to have, you're going to start smaller.

Think local: The bottom line is that it's so much easier to get on local TV versus a big national program. Local TV stations are always looking for time to fill because they have a smaller area from which to pull, whereas, national TV shows have access to nearly any expert or celebrity they want, and they have the entire nation from which to pull (not just the thirty-mile radius around Topeka, Kansas). It's also possible that a national show needs to keep up with current events, so a segment about the best way to train your dog will easily be bumped if a national or international crisis needs to be covered. In addition to it simply being easier to get yourself booked, the stakes just aren't as high. If your first appearance doesn't go as smoothly as you had hoped, it's still possible they'll have you back. The standards may not be the same as on a national program. Mess up on national TV, and you will not be asked back to the show.

To find local stations that might be interested in your segment, just look at the options around where you live. The town where I live in Utah is so small that there were literally no local stations. I had to go as far as Salt Lake City and Las Vegas to find stations. These aren't exactly small markets, but they aren't national programs either, so I said what the heck and I gave it a try. If you live in a big market like New York City or Los Angeles, you may have to be willing to fly farther out of your area to appear. One of my first appearances on a show, *Good Things Utah* in Salt Lake City, had already jump-started my income, so I decided I'd be willing to fly to any other market within two hours of my home. This opened up a ton of markets. And frankly, if you want to be an entrepreneur who makes millions of dollars, flying for two hours ultimately isn't that big a sacrifice. And once you see how lucrative doing a television appearance can be, you'll be happy to jump on a plane.

Creating a television presence takes time. When I was starting out, I often reminded myself that when an intelligence officer is working on an operation it can take months just to spot a potential asset. After a while with no major leads, a spy will often reevaluate his approach. Am I hanging out in the right areas? Am I following the right leads? Remain patient during this process, but if you're not getting any hits at all from your emails, reevaluate your approach. Try a new subject headline, tweak your jaw-dropper, rewrite your email, or try a different market.

Identify the right producers: Once you've made a list of all the stations to which you'd like to pitch your segment, you need to find the contact information for the segment producer who books people on the show. The question you'll need to ask yourself is whether you want to spend money on this part of the process or you want to take the free route. The free route works, but it can be time consuming. Check out the website for each station and search for the contact information for the segment producer or the booking producer (they're the same thing). Sometimes you'll be able to get only a generic email address, like info@newstation.com. If that's the case, you'll have to send your pitch letter to that email address and wait.

If you have the budget to fork out some cash, you can invest in a subscription service for media contact information, such as Cision or Muck Rack. These services can cost anywhere from a few hundred dollars a month to several thousand dollars a year. The benefit to using such services is that they have up-to-date contact information for hundreds of thousands of media contacts. You can find segment producers, magazine editors, newspaper editors—any kind of media contact you might want. Whatever route works best for you, once you've collected your list of producers and email addresses, whatever you do, don't email them. You can't email the producer of a show out of the blue and expect them to book you. You need to craft the perfect pitch email.

Write a pitch email that a producer will actually read: Creating a pitch email that will actually get read isn't incredibly hard. Simply put, a well-written, carefully crafted, and personal pitch email will often get read. What won't get read? A generic email that opens "Dear Sirs" or "To whom it may concern." Nor will anyone read a verbose, overly long letter that doesn't get to the point. It's also crucial that you tout your skills and credibility right away. You have to realize that segment producers get tons of emails every single day. Even local news station producers get flooded with emails on a daily basis from people who want to be on their show. I follow these simple rules every time I craft a new pitch email, and I've received a ton of responses.

RULE #1:
CRAFT A POWERFUL SUBJECT HEADLINE

If it's enticing, a producer (or, more likely, their intern or assistant) will open the email. I am grateful that I am now in the position to be able to start mine with "*New York Times* bestselling author." But before I wrote a book, I had luck with the following types of subject lines. They are straight to the point, show a sense of urgency, and immediately give the producer an idea of what I do:

> "Ex-CIA Officer Reveals Spy Secrets to Survive Kidnappings"
> "Former CIA Officer Reveals 3 Halloween Tips to Keep Kids Safe"
> "Former CIA Officer in Town—2 Days Only"
> "Former CIA Officer Leaks Home Defense Secrets for Tempe Residents"

RULE #2:
TAILOR YOUR PITCH SPECIFICALLY TO EACH SHOW

This is critical. Open with a personalized comment about their program. Something along the lines of: "Tom, I'm a huge fan of *Good Morning Wisconsin*. The segments you've been doing lately on fly fishing are really great."

RULE #3: GET TO YOUR POINT

You want to keep the email rather short. Don't make a producer dig around looking for what they want. If someone doesn't immediately know why you're emailing, your message will get dumped in the trash. These producers do not and will not read a five-page email about how great you are and why you should be on their show.

"The reason I'm emailing you is that home break-ins are on the rise, and I'm a former CIA officer who has four simple ideas that will keep home owners safe."

RULE #4: NEVER INCLUDE ATTACHMENTS

A producer isn't going to open your attachment. Opening an attachment quite simply is more work for them. Chances are they'll stop reading your email and dump it in the trash. Critical information about you or your segment must be in the body of the email.

RULE #5: INCLUDE LINKS TO YOUR ACHIEVEMENTS

It's fine to include links to any articles that have been written about you or previous television appearances. These should be mentioned in the email as well.

RULE #6: ESTABLISH A DEADLINE

Include a deadline in your email to add urgency and make them want to get in touch with you. This is a small push—so don't be a jerk about it. A deadline is "I'm available these dates" or "I'm in town the following week." Saying something harsh, like "If you want me to be on your show I need to hear from you within 24 hours," is definitely *not* going to get you on TV.

SPLIT TEST YOUR SUBJECT LINES

Spend time crafting two strong subject lines. If you have an email list of a thousand people, send subject line A to half the list and B to the other half. Instead of pitching a TV segment, you'll be pitching the item you sell or your service. After you send out the emails, note which subject line gets the better response rate. You can also note which one gets a better click-through rate and generates more sales. The subject line that creates the most action is your winner—ding, ding, ding. My email list is currently comprised of 190,000 people and I am constantly split testing subject lines for every product I send out.

PUT IT ALL TOGETHER

Obviously, you should craft an email that you feel best represents who you are, why you should be on TV, and why your jaw-dropper is a must-see for their TV audience. I've attached a sample email I've written (and it works) to give you an idea of what it all looks like in the end:

WINNING SUBJECT LINE

Email Subject Line: *New York Times* Bestselling Ex-CIA Officer

Hi, Julie,

My name is Jason Hanson.

I'm a former CIA Officer and the *New York Times* bestselling author of *Spy Secrets That Can Save Your Life.*

On September 4–6, I'll be in Denver on a business trip and I'll be about 7 miles from your station.

I teach people spy secrets of how to escape duct tape if they're ever kidnapped. (Duct tape is the #1 way in which people are kidnapped all over the world.)

It's an exciting segment that people love to watch, and I think your hosts and viewers would find it fun and beneficial.

I can also share little-known home defense tips based on CIA safe houses. (Unfortunately, there were over 53,400 home burglaries in Denver last year.)

You can see my bio here: https://spyescapeandevasion.com/ jason-hanson-biography/

You can see my past TV appearances here: https:// spyescapeandevasion.com/press/

Please let me know if you have any questions. My schedule is open to come on your show the morning of September 5 or September 6 if it's possible and would work for you.

Thank you for your time.

Sincerely,

Jason Hanson

[My email address here]

[My cell phone here]

[PRO TIPS]

THE EXTRA PUSH

If you've followed the rules carefully, there's an excellent chance you will receive a response in just a few days. If you don't, you should do an extra push. An extra push is just a follow-up email that dials up the urgency a little bit. Whenever I've had to do an extra push, I've included a line such as . . .

> Hi Julie,
>> I don't want you to miss this . . .
>> Jason Hanson here.
>> I'm a former CIA Officer and the New York Times bestselling author of Spy Secrets That Can Save Your Life.

OTHER EXAMPLES OF LINES THAT CAN HELP DIAL UP THE URGENCY MAY INCLUDE:

- "My school safety tactics can save a child's life today."
- "Muggings in the area have doubled in the last month."
- "Fifty percent of people aren't prepared for the approaching hurricane season."

HOW TO DOMINATE YOUR FIRST TELEVISION APPEARANCE AND GET ASKED BACK FOR ANOTHER APPEARANCE

Congratulations. You've booked your first television appearance at a local station. If played right, this appearance could open up an entirely new chapter in your life—and can bring in endless income for your business. For what it's worth, I was a little nervous when I did my first television segment on *Good Things Utah*. While I always do as much research as I can before embarking on something new, I would have welcomed tips from someone who had done it before. Producers love it when you make their lives easier, and they have reliable, interesting, trustworthy people whom they can pull out of their back pocket to make an appearance. My goal was to be a producer's go-to choice for segments on safety and survival.

To make things easier for you and your journey upward, I've compiled what I've observed to be the best tips to make a guest a desirable choice to be on TV. If you make sure to incorporate the following tips into your first appearance, you'll do great, and chances are you'll be asked back again.

Dress the part: I always wear a black suit and tie on television. I feel this is what people expect from a former intelligence officer. While I'd love to show up in jeans and a T-shirt, that wouldn't exude an air of reliability. I'm not saying everyone needs to wear a suit. If your expertise falls into an area where it would be appropriate for you to wear fun, less formal clothing, then go for it. Just make sure you look like the expert you want to be perceived to be.

Arrive early: Arriving late for a television appearance is
a total disaster. The segments are perfectly timed, and
showing up late will instantly mess up the producer's
schedule—and you'll never be asked back. On national
television they are so careful about timing that they'll
send a car for you to ensure you won't get lost. Sometimes
a show will do this even if you're just a few blocks away.
If you don't know the area, drive the route in advance. If
you're flying, arrive the day before if possible. Give yourself
more time than you would ever need to make it to the
studio.

Double-check your props: Never assume the studio will
have what you need for your segment. Bring everything
with you and bring extras. If you have items that require
batteries, bring an additional set. The intelligence officer
in me is always overly prepared, and being prepared for
television appearances ensures that nothing will go wrong.
Knowing you have everything you need is an antidote to
the swell of nerves.

Don't be starstruck: As you continue to build your media
presence and start doing national shows, you'll eventually
encounter an A List celebrity in the green room. When this
happens, just say hello and mind your own business—even
if it's your favorite musician of all time. The worst thing
you can do is behave like an annoying fan who pesters
them. If they want to talk to you, they'll let you know.

I was in the green room one time with another guest
who wouldn't stop talking to a celebrity. When the
producer walked in, the celeb gave him a look that said,
"Get this guy away from me." Producers want A List

celebrities to come back on their show, so if you turn out to be the kind of guest that can't leave such people alone, you won't be asked back.

It's like a chat between two good friends: When it's your time to go on the air, you'll be escorted to the set. The guy operating the camera will give you the countdown. Once the segment goes live, the host will look directly at the camera and read the teleprompter to introduce you. During this time, you should also look directly at the camera and smile. After you've been introduced the host will turn to you, and that's your signal to start sharing your information with the audience. Talk to the host, not the camera. It's exactly like two friends having a casual conversation. Forget the camera is even there. Continue with your segment exactly as you practiced it. When you finish, the host will again look back to the camera and mention your book, product, or service before teasing out the next segment.

When you're done, you're out: Once you go off the air, someone will come and remove your microphone and the producer with whom you've been working will escort you out. It's a fast and businesslike process. Don't think that you're going to hang around and that they're going to sit and chat with you. Shows are very fast paced—it's organized chaos—and they've got to go right to the next segment.

HOW TO TURN ONE SEGMENT
INTO MULTIPLE SEGMENTS

Hopefully all went well and all of that practice paid off. If you did your job well, you showed up on time, behaved in a professional manner, and delivered a great segment—and chances are you'll be asked back. If I see the producer I worked with on my way out, I'll thank them for having me on and tell them I have several other ideas that would make great segments. Oftentimes they'll ask you back before you even bring it up.

> **The self-critique:** I always want to improve, so I carefully critique my own television appearances once I receive a copy of the recording. One time I sat with my legs stretched out, which, upon review, just looked terrible. I made a point of making sure I never sat that way again. I also paid attention to my pacing, voice, and vocabulary. Once you have the opportunity to see your appearance, note the following:
> - Did your outfit look right for the appearance? Would you change anything about it next time?
> - Did you speak clearly and at an appropriate volume?
> - Were there any filler words that you need to avoid next time? Did you say "mm" between lines?
> - How was your posture?
> - Could your pacing improve? Did you speak too quickly or too slowly?
> - Was your demonstration clear and jaw-dropping, as it needs to be to wow an audience?
> - Were your props appropriate and clearly visible?

The value-added follow-up: Ideally, a producer will be in touch and ask you about other segment ideas. If not, you should send a follow-up email within the next couple of days. Either way, it's important that you respond with multiple segment ideas. You want to give a producer a variety of choices that show off what you're capable of doing. One great reason to send multiple ideas is that if a national show has to fly you out, it's possible they would shoot more than one segment. That's a win for everyone. Following is an example of a follow-up email I sent that got me asked back on a show several times:

[FIRST NAME,]

Thank you so much for having me on your show. Following are several more ideas for a segment. Let me know if you need more. Thank you.

1. THE IMPROVISED WEAPON: There are a lot of places you can't bring weapons, such as an airplane. But one thing you can do is to carry a can of soda and a sock. If you feel you are in danger, you can drop the can of soda into the sock, and if you smack someone with it, it will do some serious damage. It might be fun to put a can in a sock and let [HOST NAME] take some whacks at something (not at me). Perhaps swinging down on a wooden table so you can hear the thud of the can.

2. HOW TO STOP AN ATTACKER WHO GRABS YOUR HAIR FROM BEHIND: Criminals commonly do this to women when they follow them through a parking lot to their car. I can show the simple move a woman can use to get away from an attacker who grabs her hair.

3. USING A CANE AS A WEAPON: As people get older they often have to rely on canes, and these can be taken anywhere. I could show some simple moves with the cane, such as where to strike a person to create that window of opportunity to get away.

4. HOW TO ESCAPE A HEADLOCK: There's a simple move to escape if a criminal puts you in a headlock and tries to repeatedly punch you.

5. WHAT TO DO IF SOMEONE HAS YOU ON THE GROUND AND IS ON TOP OF YOU: This would be a more awkward position but it would likely be a hilarious visual and make the audience laugh. So [HOST NAME] and I would be in a wrestling position. [HOST] would be on the ground, I would be on top as if I was an attacker, I would show how to stop me.

Jason

You can see that I gave the producers several ideas from which to choose. Don't just send them a single idea. You want to make it as easy as possible for them to find an idea they like so they will have you back on the show. Remember, each appearance on a show means extra money in your pocket.

ACKNOWLEDGMENTS

I'm incredibly grateful to the mentors I've had who truly are the best spies and salesmen in the world. (Especially, for the wisdom about getting out of precarious situations that life throws your way—*"You can talk your way out, walk your way out, or risk not getting out."*)

This book would not exist without the efforts of many people. Thank you to my editor, Matthew Daddona, for your dedication, hard work, and diligence. I'd also like to thank everyone else at Dey Street for making this book a reality: Lynn Grady, Carrie Thornton, Kendra Newton, Alison Hinchcliffe, Kelly Rudolph, Benjamin Steinberg, David Palmer, Nyamekye Waliyaya, Andrea Molitor, Melanie Bedor, Suet Chong, Renata De Oliveira, and Ploy Siripant. Thank you to my agent, Kirsten Neuhaus at Foundry, and Paula Balzer for helping me execute my vision. And as always, thank you to my wonderful wife, Amanda, I'd never get anything done without your support. Lastly, thank you to the incredible men and women of the CIA who work tirelessly to protect our great nation.

ABOUT THE AUTHOR

Jason R. Hanson is a former CIA Officer, *New York Times* best-selling author, and serial entrepreneur. He runs a marketing company that helps entrepreneurs grow their businesses and he also runs a survival company. Jason resides in Cedar City, Utah, with his family and can be reached through www.Spy masterBook.com.